Discovering Life

A Poet Within

Discovering Life

A Poet Within

Maj Gen Purshotam Vig
AVSM, VSM (Retd)

Vitasta

Vitasta Publishing Pvt. Ltd.
New Delhi

Published by
Vitasta Publishing Pvt. Ltd.
2/15, Ansari Road, Daryaganj,
New Delhi - 110 002
info@vitastapublishing.com

ISBN: 978-93-80828-46-6

Cover Design and Layout by Vitasta Publishing Pvt. Ltd.
Printed by Vits Press, New Delhi

To My Family

Contents

Section-II
Someone Somewhere

Section-III
Light for My Soul

Preface

My urge to discover the mystery of life and the reality of living deepened when I ventured to share my thoughts in my first book, *Seasons of Life, Extraordinary Life of an Ordinary Soldier.* The book was biographical in nature, but with a difference. It was an anthology of my thoughts and observations about various facets of life interwoven with my experiences. It was heartening to see that it came out to be highly readable and was well received, transcending the barriers of age, sex and borders.

After submitting the manuscript to the publishers, I had ample time at my disposal. I could read more and refresh my thoughts. But little did I know that the urge to share my thoughts had kindled an insatiable desire in me to write. Writing had become my passion. Now, in one stroke, this activity was over. The void so created was gripping and gave rise to a hollow feeling within. Many conflicting thoughts churned in my mind. Many questions surfaced. What next? Where to proceed thence? Was I done with writing? Had I said it all? Had my thoughts dried? More I read and re-read my manuscript, the more I was convinced that in my quest on matters of life, I had barely touched the tip of the iceberg. There was so much more to read, learn, observe and experience. Ideas were effervescent in the cauldron but were muddled in a chaos. The urge to write continued to tickle my mind. But I was clueless about the direction. And then flashed a thought. Eureka moment it was for me.

My family group, who had vetted my manuscripts, gave me the impression that I had a natural style of writing, verging on the poetic. My thoughts flowed straight from the heart. This rang a bell. The seed had been planted. It germinated only after some serious thinking. *Complete Works of Shakespeare* was one of the books that I was reading at that time. I was enthralled by his style and expression, what I learnt later, was in the *blank verse*. Finally, the trigger. It came from *Geeetanjli,* by Rabindranath Tagore. Inspired by works of these great masters, I decided to test the unknown waters and took the plunge into the unfathomable depth of the alternate form of expression, the artistic domain of poetry.

I wrote my first poem, *Glory to Ye O Moon*. With great reluctance, I circulated it to my family group. The response was very encouraging. The next ones, *In Remembrance, I am Ever in Competition* and *What was My Fault*, were instantaneous hits. This overwhelming response put paid to all the turmoil within. I had found my direction. Thus started this odyssey. Following my instincts and compassion I found my thoughts in full flow to write on various facets of life, this time in poetry. This was the beginning of a strange but pleasant transformation for me.

A senior army officer with four decades of military life, highly decorated, adventurous, a sportsman of some standing, now a veteran but still active, turned an author, daring to venture into poetry, a preserve of the literary intellectuals. My stomach churned. How would it be? Would I be accepted? I was not sure. But I had fallen in love with this form of expression, I could not hold back. I took my chances and went ahead.

With passage of time, I wrote on many themes. Love and romance, the pain of separation and yearning for the loved one. This sublime feeling of surrender is unique and is central to the human mind. I am beholden to nature and its manifestations and how these impact us. I stand in awe and gratitude to this mighty cosmic force. I have relished dealing with many facets of nature, the joy and strength that we derive from these and pain and misery that these are capable of unleashing.

Pain and misery are the realities of human life. These arouse our compassion and demand that empathy be an essential part of our attitude, to be alive to the problems of others and then to reach out and extend a benign hand of comfort in any form. Conflicting thoughts, dilemmas within, the memories and wish lists, all form a vital part of our psyche. I have tried to tackle many of these issues. Poetry can never be complete without stretching our imagination beyond the barriers of thought. I have done so in many poems, including attempting to crystal gaze into my life, in this life and the life after, in dealing with a thought-provoking dispensation -- to carry a hand bag to the next world and all that one would like to carry along.

This journey has not been as smooth as it appears or the impression that I may have given. There were stages, particularly in the second half, when I found fresh thoughts eluding me. My mind would go blank. I had to but wait for the thoughts to resurface. I would often withdraw to my solitude and look within. Sooner or later, fresh springs would sprout. I have captured this theme in the poem, *Have My Thoughts Dried.* At the end of this journey, here I am with a collection of 100 poems. All on different topics. All about various facets of life, all with a subtle message and all in the first person, placing my head on the block. This was not done with a design, but has emerged to be so. Perhaps, instinctively.

I would like to share with my readers, that it is only after having written quite a few poems that I went into the how and why of writing a poem. The styles, the discipline and its various forms. I took shelter in a wonderful format, the free verse. It gives a carte blanche to write the way one wants to. This freedom is unique and frees one from any rules and regulations. But the fundamental issue remains. It is the thought which matters and not the way one has stylized it. Alliterations, metaphors, rhythm and rhyme, no doubt add spice to the expression but vital is the thought behind the thought. This new-found freedom enriches the mind and empowers anyone and everyone to be poetic. I will be naïve to say that I did not gain from formal forms of poetry. I did revisit all my poems and tried to refine these. But I did not tamper with my initial thoughts, nor did I change my style. What I present is pure as the first thoughts that came to my mind. While I am reluctant to consider myself worthy of the company of exalted poets, I have come to realise that there is a poet residing within each one's mind, waiting for a call or an opportunity. I have captured this thought in my poem, *A Poet Within*. This is my expression about life, as I have observed and experienced. It is this expression that I wish to share with my readers. All pure and innocent and straight from the heart.

Purshotam Vig
Maj Gen (Retd)

Introduction

'Discovering Life, A Poet Within' is a collection of 100 poems by a former army officer, turned an author and now a poet. The book is a flow of his thoughts in his attempt to unravel the mystery of life. This mystery, so close to our hearts, yet so distant. The mystery, though it appears simple and transparent, remains hidden under layers of unpredictability, uncertainty and multiplicity. One may unravel some, yet another layer continues to shroud the thought. Many thinking minds have devoted their lifetime in the quest for the truth. Yet numerous answers remain unanswered. So what is all this mystery about?

The book weaves us through the web of various facets of life and their attendant sensitivities, the pleasure and the pain. *Sublime feeling of love* for the beloved and the Master, the inspiration it conjures, the pain of separation, longing for the beloved, blindness in love and fantasy in love are some of the themes. Some of the poems being, The First Love, describing the power of the first love, the helplessness of those affected and the beauty of even having loved and lost than not to have loved at all. Yet another, Could it Happen, fantasizes the bliss in every thought of the beloved, only if she would appear unexpectedly and surprise him yet again. The author relates to the bliss of the moments stolen in the company of his love, in Those Stolen Moments and in admiring the power of her gaze, in Those Eyes. Yet some more poems like And Then We Drifted Away, I Waited for Thee, and I Await Thy Reply, deal with the pain of separation in love. Someone Somewhere is a beautiful thought. The author feels there is someone waiting for him somewhere. Someone whose heart beats for him. He is in a constant quest of this 'someone' and lives in hope…

The author picks up threads from the present and the past and a vision about the future in many of his poems. *Memories* are central to life. One may reminisce, but there is bound to be pain in some of the memories. Having left his nest at a very young age, the author is particularly alive to the sensitive feeling of his early years. He deals with this theme in many of his poems, like, My Fading Memory, Am I a Stranger, The Moorings, Reminiscences, How Green Was My Valley and so on.

Fantasizing about *the future* appears in many of the poems, some being, Crystal Gazing about the future and the futility of it. The Hand Bag is a beautiful dream, if one was allowed a hand bag to the next world, what all one would like to carry. Yet another, Why Not Just Pretend. This theme gives a whole new meaning to life. Only if one could pretend a little, then one would be happy and content all the time. And perhaps, after some time the very need to pretend would disappear. If I Had a Choice is a poem fusing the aspirations and the reality of life. It dwells on the wish list of a naïve mind. Once the truth dawns, it is overwhelmed by anguish for being selfish, seeking everything for himself and nothing for those in misery around.

The book deals with another vital facet of life, *pain and misery.* Inquisitive by nature and with deep compassion in heart, the author is overwhelmed by misery in life, for what he observes around.

These thoughts manifest touchingly in many of his poems. What Was My Fault is a touching poem unfolding the observations of a deprived child, who relishes all niceties of life, but from a distance and her one innocent but unanswerable query. Yet another, I Am a Dalit, the thoughts of a naïve child of a dalit family, his aspirations, and queries to the world. The Security Guard, on his travails, the disorientation due to lack of sleep, frugal life and his helplessness to extricate himself from this quagmire. The Railways Station is yet another real life issue faced by millions of poor, particularly the daily wagers, who are forced by their poverty to leave their home and hearth for greener pastures, only to find these otherwise. Even at the cost of loss of wages and job, the necessity to travel home and their travails for the travel. A scene at a busy and congested railway junction is an eye opener and heartrending.

Another theme this book dwells on is on the thoughts which are *a stretch of his imagination* and if these thoughts were to come true. In his poem, Wings, admiring elegant and graceful flock of geese glide past in a formation, the author dreams, how the life would be if he too were to have wings and freedom to move at will. What a wonderful turn life could take. He goes on to stretch his thoughts, why him only, why not all. So many problems of life would be solved. He urges the Lord to at least give this thought a try. He is enthralled by the marine life. In his poem, The Fish, he traces the graceful movements of a school of fish, and visualizes how would it be to be a fish. He also imagines if his love too would take the plunge. They would swim, side by side, under water, until…

The author is beholden to *nature and its cosmic manifestation* in varied forms. His poems, O Ye Setting Sun, Glory to Ye O Moon, The Wind, The Snow Flakes, A Mountain Stream and The Eclipse beautifully trace these rich and awesome phenomena. He respects nature for the control that it exercises on our lives, be these through the cycle of the seasons or the rain, with their attendant impact on one and all. Some of the poems covering these phenomena are, The Scorching Sun of May, which elucidates the unbearable heat but necessity for many to still be outdoors and to work suffering this cosmic wrath. Similarly, O Ye Winter is a poem about winter, which though is shortening in its span due to global warming, can sometimes be treacherous. The Autumn unfurls a different view about this unwelcome season. The author loves the romanticism of rain and brings it out in his poems, Soothing Patter of the Rain and The first Shower of the Monsoon.

The dilemma of *conflicting thoughts* is another theme of many poems in this book. The Conflict Within, brings out the dilemma of the present and the past. The sub and the conscious mind. The floating state of the mind, the state in which one dreams and is creative. Similarly, At the Cross Roads I Stand deals with yet another facet of conflicting thoughts.

In almost all the poems, there is a subtle message hidden on the reality of this life. The author does not claim to be a poet, but feels that there is a poet residing in each one of us, waiting to emerge at the opportune time and given an appropriate trigger. This book derives its name from this very thought and so does his poem, The Poet Within. Intricate thoughts about the poetic domain are neatly woven in this poem. One simple message that takes shape is, 'it is the thoughts which matter and the flow, rules and regulations don't regulate this show'. He feels that, it is the compassion and sensitivity which create the flow, 'being a poet is not the domain of a chosen few, there is a poet in each one of us, waiting to take a view'.

Overall, the book is his quest for discovery of life, through love and compassion, picking up threads about myriad facets of life. It is a saga of his odyssey to perceive life. Sensitivity to life and his empathic mind richly bring out the thoughts that one may relate to. The author has dared to dabble in intricate topics like, tracing the life of a diamond in Am I for Ever, of mankind in But for Noah's Ark, the phenomenon of snow in The Snow Flakes and many more. Each topic has been well researched and beautifully interwoven with his poetic thoughts. It is a book readable by one and all, irrespective of age, sex and nationality. There is so much to pick up from this book.

Acknowledgements

This book is not a book. It is the story of my journey in an unknown territory. It is the sum total of my thoughts and expression in a totally new language. The language of love and warmth. The language in which the author plays with words, the rhythm and the rhyme, arousing the sentiments of the readers, verging on a crescendo. The language, I learnt, absorbed and ventured to imbibe. The language of poetry. I was not totally new to this form of expression. I had cursorily read some poems. But I had never read these with a focus, nor had I imagined even in my dreams that I will be knocking at the doors of such a wonderful phenomenon, seeking entry, so late in life. But it has happened.

This book would not have been there, but for the support and encouragement of many of my well wishers. I stand indebted to them for triggering the fire in my belly and initiating me to this wonderful world of poetry. The world, which I always considered to be a forbidden domain. Domain of the chosen few. The literary wizards. Little did I know that there is a poet residing in each one of us, waiting to step out. But all these revelations came only as I went along, writing my poems. The most difficult part was the start and to get my own confidence. Later, it became vital to get some level of acceptance. Once I had gained a foothold, then I was on the roll. Ideas did flow. My mind soared. All this until the plateau reached. And then there was a sudden lull. My mind went blank. Blank in stare, I shuddered with fright. Had my thoughts dried? Was this all? Would I be able to proceed at all, or I would have to abandon this massive effort, which had, incidentally become my first love. But then my solitude came to my rescue. I retracted to my shell, focused and refreshed my thoughts, allowing my inner springs to sprout. With time these did, and with encouragement from my core group, which essentially is my family group, I bounced back. This book therefore, is not my show alone. I may have been the conduit to think and write, but nothing would have materialized, but for the unstinted support, inspiration and encouragement from many quarters.

I owe my existence and values to my parents, both now in their heavenly abode. I am deeply grateful to the members of my family, my wife, son and daughter, their spouses and my sister. They formed my core group for this project. I acknowledge the support of my wife in providing me with an environment, conducive for this creative activity. She gave me the first feedback on my writings. I am thankful to our daughter and daughter-in-law, for their support and encouragement. Excited like a child, I would eagerly wait for their responses, which would invariably be prompt, in spite of their own busy schedule. I valued their responses, as I felt that women have a soft corner for poetry. Response from our son has been very important and vital for me, as it would reflect the male view, typically of the modern and young generation. I credit my sister for innocuously planting the thought of my potential to write poetry. The idea remained in my subconscious mind, but has finally fructified. I am grateful to our son-in-law, for his vital contribution in suggesting many of the themes when my thoughts ran dry.

I am indebted to my teachers at all levels, particularly in my formative years, for triggering the urge in me to seek knowledge. I owe my gratitude to the National Defence Academy, my alma mater, for transforming a raw adolescent like me into a vibrant young officer and strengthening the basic tenets and values. I salute the elite Indian Army and within that, my own department, the Corps of Electronics and Mechanical Engineers, in nurturing me for nearly four decades and transforming me from a young officer to a mature and a thinking mind.

I am grateful to my publishers and their editorial staff for their whole-hearted support and painstaking effort in breathing life into this work.

Reading *The Complete Works of William Shakespeare* has been an intellectual experience. His power of expression, subtle humour, and ability to make his characters come alive is awesome. His writing has been the primary source of inspiration for me. I stand with my head bowed to the great master. *Geetanjli,* the masterpiece of Rabindranath Tagore, has left an indelible mark on me. His work has touched my heart. It has been the trigger for me to start this journey. I am deeply impressed by the great poet John Milton and his work, *Paradise Lost*, which I am still reading. His writing has given a new direction to my expression. Inspired by his work, I have written the poem, *But for Noah's Ark*. I have read some works of Rudyard Kipling and admire him for his great poem of all times, If. The theme of this poem has been a source of inspiration for me, in my formative years and even later. Once I had finished my manuscript, I then read poems of famous poets like William Wordsworth, John Keats, George Eliot, Edgar Allen Poe, Oscar Wilde and many others. The aim was also to assess my own writing. Initial reading of my work after this gave me a hollow feeling. I had to revisit my poems many times. Finally, I have reached, where I stand today. I, therefore, am thankful to all these great masters, as their works have helped me refine my poems. At the same time, I must also state that I did not tamper with my style. These remain pure, as in the original form.

I am thankful to the internet, the web media and Google. But for them, I would have been totally stranded. I am particularly indebted to Wikipedia, their elaborate network and research on so many subjects. I have fallen back on them often for clarification of my thoughts on many issues. I continue to be grateful to Bill Gates, for his Microsoft Office, without which, I would have never been able to proceed.

Some thoughts and facts, which appear in these Acknowledgements above and in the write up, About The Author, in this book, are common to those, in my first book, *Seasons of Life, Extraordinary Life of an Ordinary Soldier*. These pertain to me as a person and are equally true for both the books.

Finally, I wish to state that whilst I have browsed various sites, read many poets, the work and the thoughts in this book are totally mine. If there is a resemblance in any form, to any one else's work, in part, or in full, it is purely unintentional and inadvertent, which if brought to my notice, I will unhesitatingly rectify.

About the Author

Maj Gen Purshotam Vig, AVSM, VSM (Retd) was born in 1944 in the picturesque town of Baramulla, in the state of Jammu and Kashmir. Followed by turbulent initial years, he surprised himself by opting for and making it to the elite National Defence Academy. He was commissioned in the then Corps of Electrical and Mechanical Engineers of the Indian Army in 1964. In the course of his eventful career spanning nearly four decades, he acquired high-end qualifications both in the technical and executive channels. He held many key and prestigious command, staff and instructional appointments both in his own discipline and on the general staff. A rare honour for a technical stream officer. Focused on his profession, he would still find time to pursue his interests in reading and in the outdoors.

A qualified engineer, the author holds masters in three varying disciplines: Electronics (communications) from the Army, Business Administration and Defence Studies. Besides, he is an alumnus of the Defence Services Staff College, Wellington, Higher Command Course, College of Combat, now the Army War College and a fellow of many prestigious technical institutions.

He was conferred with the Presidential awards for distinguished services, namely, Vishisht Seva Medal following command of the battalion in 1985, and Ati Vishisht Seva Medal for his contributions in the operationally-active scenario in the Northern Command as a Major General. In addition, he was awarded the Commendation Card by the

Chief of the Army Staff for his contributions in a strike formation as a Brigadier in 1994. On the extracurricular front, he is an adventurist, loves nature and outdoor life. He qualified as a paratrooper and was a part of the elite parachute formation. The author has been and still is a keen squash player, an ardent golfer and a proficient yachtsman. He has fair achievements in these sports to his credit, including having represented the country in yachting.

He has an inquisitive mind and is a keen observer of life. His urge to go deeper into the philosophy of life has triggered his passion to diversify his reading in many directions, giving him an insight into various facets of life. He is a unique combination of an intellectual mind, an adventure-lover and above all a man full of compassion. His achievements in varied fields are a rare mix. He was considered to be a source of inspiration and a role-model by many.

His passion for wide range of reading and his rich experiences in life were a natural precursor to sharing his thoughts and experiences with others. Towards this end he authored a highly readable book, '*Seasons of Life, Extraordinary Life of an Ordinary Soldier*'. The book was released in a glittering ceremony in June 2010. Many felt that reading the book was an educative experience. They found the book to be inspirational, instructive and interesting. Overwhelmed by the wide acceptance and the feed back received, the author made an honest effort to reach the youth and sent complimentary copies to virtually the entire hierarchy in the army, to numerous schools, training institutions, libraries, universities, besides to many luminaries across the country. The response to this effort has been awesome. His writing style is simple. Thoughts flow as if straight from the heart. Some felt he had a poetic style. Hence his next venture to pen his thoughts, again on matters of life, this time not in prose, but in poetry.

He hung his uniform in 2002 and lives with his wife in Panchkula, India. He actively continues with his literary pursuits, besides regular squash and golf.

Section – I

Discovering Myself

1
Discovering Myself

Who am I, why am I, often surfaces the thought
I seek the answer, I grope, I am lost, I am distraught
I read, I research, I ask, but none offer me a pointed reply
so common a query yet unknown, to all, does it equally apply;

Am I an enigma, am I soft, am I hard, what am I in my crust
am I emotive, am I romantic, am I worthy of someone's trust
am I tall, am I short, am I full or else hollow in my thought
am I empathic, am I outreaching, have I compassion in my heart;

I think, I reflect, I debate, wither the answers, so basic, yet none
I feel foolish, life well spent, so much gone, ever been on the run
what have I done and what for, have I whiled away my time
why and how of mine I know not, nothing short of a crime;

Enough is enough, I decide to unearth the myth of my life
I trace my journey down the memory lane, the struggle, strive
by piece and stage, I dig deep, I recollect from the beginning
opaque to translucent the myth turns, some light is passing;

The cloud starts to lift, my very genesis, how was I created
a thought, an incidence, a coincidence, wanted or unwanted
probability of one in millions and that too, a rare chance to be
a random creation was I, equal chance to be a he or a she;

And when I did take shape, what was I finally to be
just a body, me a nobody, with plenty of water in me
a lot of carbon, some nitrogen, oxygen, hydrogen and the rest
the soul was actually me, rest being dust, destined back to dust;

I came, I saw, I learnt the ways of life
I performed, I excelled, I rose high
I loved, I lived, I was ever in shine
time flew, soon I was past my prime;

My nitrogen has aged, my carbon too and the rest to state
my soul ever so dynamic, so difficult to hold it in the cage
eager to move to fresh pastures, none can hold it any more
anxious am I no longer to seek, the why and how of me as afore.

***

2

The Fog

The path was meandering down the dale
I still recall when thou walked down the vale
bereft of speech, I watched thee astride the path
till end of the horizon, until I lost thee in the fog;

Stunned was I, by the events all so fast
the turn in my life, as you chose to depart
low hanging envelope, suddenly so downcast
I waited in hope, for thou to emerge from the fog;

While in wait, I thought of the times together
in a world of our own, like birds of a feather
hand in hand, our walks down the path
romance in the air, filled by the fog;

What a phenomenon, O fog! we would muse
myriad forms, with mist or haze to confuse
a collection of tiny dots of ice, was thy spread
descending softly from the heavens, as if in a quest;

We would often wonder, if thou rose from the sea
or from the humid trees and plants transpiring
or were from a marsh or a lake in the vicinity
graceful were thee in thy drift, across the valley;

If dense, a mysterious shroud would thee cast
vision unable to penetrate, in thy veil, one be lost
sometimes I sit back and reflect on my past
it rekindles the fire, in thy fold, my love was lost;

I have waited in vain, but hope I have not lost
in some magic moment, the fog may lift from my heart
my love to become real, revive from my reminiscent past
and she would retrace with grace, her steps back from the fog.

***

3
The Smile

Captivating was her perfect smile
transfixed was my gaze, all the while
in a trance was I, until she was not to be
etched is that smile for ever, in my memory;

Pure and innocent is a child's smile
transparent it is, with nothing to hide
refreshing as the sunshine, is this smile
clear as sky, sans any ruse and guile;

As I step out, I confront a stranger passing by
angst on his face visible, ready to burst any time
face to face, curious was he, to find me a-smile
was it telepathy, soon, he too broke into a smile;

A wonder it is, this phenomenon of a smile
straight from the heart, triggers positive vibes
mere flexing of the facial muscle, is all this smile
but what an impact, establishes a rapport for life;

Myriad are the ways, for one to smile
from ear to ear, grin, curving the mouth slight
glow on the face, glisten in the eyes, when you smile
fills one with compassion, can transform one's life;

Smile is infectious, you smile the world smiles
it takes little effort, can melt even a harsh mind
strange are its ways, comes but natural and not by design
genuine it is, reflects happiness within, a blessing in disguise;

Time has flown, I sit back and reflect on my life
how have I been, somber or donning a smile
strange I feel, whilst life has been fast passing by
but can hardly recollect, when did I last smile
is it the restive mind or have I forgotten how to smile?

***

4
The First Love

The first love is like a ray of the rising sun
enriches the life of all, on whom it descends
innocent it is, treading on the path so pure
a wonderful feeling, the first love does conjure;

The first love, opens vistas unknown
engulfs the lovers, has a charm of its own
like a breath of fresh air, does it appear
a virgin emotion, fills excitement in the air;

If young, first love is intense and fierce
rare is this emotion, the hearts does it pierce
more stable and balanced, if comes later in life
unmindful of either, the time flies day and night;

When in love, one dreams only of love
to be with the love, to live for the love
fond are the memories, of the first love
but pain is intense, when gone is the love;

Sometimes I wonder, is first love a notion
is it mere attraction, passion or infatuation
a feeling of surrender or a sensory perception
when first love is also the last, life is an exception;

Whence the first love may lead to, one seldom does care
to be in love is what matters, response be there or not there
should it lead to a happy note, it becomes the driving force
yet one is content, to love not to be loved, but love and more;

First love is a gate crasher, it appears out of the blue
one hardly has time to think and deliberate, so true
it happens at the first glance, it beats the rationale
sends a shiver up the spine, the sensation so rare;

I sit back and reflect, is this feeling true for all
there are many not in love, it is not the end all
the passion for work too, is one form of love
the pleasure and the pain of love are, as hand in glove
yet divine is the experience of love, as they call
better to have loved and lost, than not loved at all.

***

5
The Passing Moment

Each passing moment, is a moment gone by
moment spent in love, or in wait otherwise
moments spent in pleasure, or pain in life
like an arrow, once shot, never to come by;

Each passing moment, is a sign of life
life is joy, to feel, to love, to strive
some moments slow, some are fast
but the moments of love, hardly last;

I watch the moments fondly, as they come
all in a hurry, I wish, I could hold on to some
some moments hang heavy, lasting a life time
if these too pass as due, life would be sublime;

I fondly recall my moments of glory
I had it all for real, envy of a story
success and fortunes, that one would seek
my love besides, life was, as if complete;

Only if time could stand still, it was not to be
the moments in store waiting, I could hardly see
life changed, my love gone, the glory too came to pass
but the moments continued, dragging me down to my past;

A strange thought, does cross my mind
each passing moment, is one less to find
with every moment, life is ever slipping
the count down has begun, the clock is ticking;

It is time, to take a stock of life
mixed were the moments, some not so nice
but precious have been many a moment, to care
I have had my share of moments, many of them rare;

It has been a journey, worth every moment, that passed
I lived every moment, from moment to moment, did I last
all the moments now in archives, gone to my historic past
someone may stumble across my story, lest for ever, it be lost.

***

6

Why Not Just Pretend

If I were to pretend,
all would be well, the matter would end,
bright would be each day
thrill, happiness, ever my way;

I would be ever, in a state of bliss
in love, yet thy absence, I will not miss
emotions, the agony, I will successfully hide
pretend I will, maintain a façade, with a smile;

The flowers, will ever be in bloom
seldom will be a reason, for gloom
grass will ever be green, the stream, be turbulent
the scorching sun, lashing rains, nature too could pretend;

None will be in misery, none in throes of hunger
the child will be as a child, fresh from slumber
agony of deprivation will not be on the scene
pretend if they could, minds pure, hearts would be clean;

Achievements galore, success ever my way
the level pitched high, magical would be its sway
health and wealth and plenty to spend
whether I had it all or not, I just had to pretend;

Sometimes I wonder, as if
could it all be possible, even if try one did
could success be for ever and failure for never,
if that was not to be, why miss what could never be;

Strange thoughts, often cross my mind
will there ever be enough, for one to find
what if my needs are met, to some extent
would I be content and not have to pretend;

Should success avoid me and be for ever astray
would I be in comfort, with what comes my way
I just have to look around, I am better off than many
joy is not for ever, if that be, let it be the trend
if happiness it gives, then why not just pretend.

***

7
The Silence

Wonderful were the times
you around, love was sublime
the feeling, pure and innocent
but it all changed, with your silence;

You were so close to my heart
shaken was I when you chose to depart,
did you part for a while or for good
or did you withdraw to your solitude?

You remember, we yearned for a chance
the sweet nothings and all the romance
time flew, until emerged this sudden turn
something happened and all was undone;

That silence was killing
all so noisy, yet so quiet within
one was cut off from the world and friends
nothing else mattered, only your silence loomed thence;

Was your silence suppressing your emotions,
or was it a reason for your evasion
I never could learn, even in my patience
what may my response be, to your silence;

What was it, that kept you across the hedge,
what made you shun it all and be speechless
was something weighing on your conscience
or you too were suffering, in your silence;

Life has gone by
I close my eyes
I too have learnt to peep
in my inner silence, so deep;

Will your silence ever be broken
will there be a reprieve, even as a token
will the riddle of your silence ever be resolved
in silence I remain, but unable to envisage.

***

8
The Poet Within

There is struggle within
myriad ideas, thoughts jostling
the poet in me raring to go
to unleash the powerful flow;

But the struggle continues to persist
I know not, how to control and resist
the ideas are many, but am unable to express
I scribble at random, am unhappy and depressed;

I know not, how to create a rhythm or a rhyme
I know not, how to express the depth of my mind
I know not, how to interweave a metaphor or to alliterate
disillusioned and miserable, inclined to give up, so to state;

I shake myself out of this negative vibe
I recline in the chair and close my eyes
do I have the passion and urge to write
I collect my thoughts, am ready to strike;

Ironic though, what comes to the fore
vital is what to express, how to, is not so
it is the thoughts which matter and the flow
rules and regulations don't regulate this show;

It is all about sensitivity and compassion
being natural, purity leaves an impression
being a poet is not the domain of a chosen few
there is a poet in each one of us, waiting to take a view;

The poetry is wild, free, unfettered, like a bird it flies
rhythm or rhyme if there, make it tastier as the spice
to be metaphoric, alliterative, is not the realm of all
it is the thought behind the thought, that touches the heart;

Refreshed, reassured, I continue to write, in my humble way
nurturing my thoughts, I write in verse, or in prose, so to say
I struggle not how to express, but how to keep my mind fresh
with time I too will learn, to interweave the style and the rest.

***

9

Are You For Real

Are you for real, or a stretch of my imagination
so far, so elusive, you triggered my transformation
with you in my thought, my life did come alive
you became my raison d'être, the reason to survive;

My eyes wandering in the crowd, seeking you, I envisage
you remained ephemeral, your image fleeting, as in a mirage
sometimes I could sense, fondly probing, was your stare
but appear you never did, staying discreetly, from the glare;

How and when started this game of hide and seek, I know not
you were ever in my dream, embedded deep, in my thought
though distant, but you became my source of inspiration
I continue to wonder, so much strength, from mere imagination;

I wait in patience, wondering, is it love, if so, platonic it may be
how could you refresh my life, your presence, virtual be indeed
thinking of you, I have gone ahead with my chores
adrenaline flowing, achievements many and yet more;

Stray thoughts do cross my mind, as I close my eyes to reflect
if you were for real, the joy, I would hardly be able to suppress
I stretch my imagination, how life would be, with you beside
you, now no longer unreal, will I be at rest, or otherwise;

Will love be aflame for ever and life be bright
once sheen of the thrill wears off, will the fire still be alight
will the mind be still, the heart satisfied and content
or the urge will surface yet again, unreal may be the real intent;

Why this turbulence in thought, it was only a fantasy
to think of you from unreal to real a stretch of prophecy
it was not to be, nor did this happen
I continued to live, in a world of my imagination
I know you are there somewhere, near or far
to recall you, I don't have to go too far
I just close my eyes and there you are;

Now that life has gone by, I stand on the edge
a step away from this long journey, just across the ledge
when I go, will you be there too, in person or in imagination
the soul lives, I believe in destiny, now also in reincarnation.

***

10

Am I My Own Soul

Who am I, what am I, why am I, I often enquire
am I the body, the atman, a thought or the senses' desire
am I of this world or the world beyond, near or far
am I corporeal, a passing cloud or permanent beyond all;

Am I born when embodied, or conceived as a tiny cell
infusing life in the sentient and the non, a story to tell
I reside in this biological attire, until when I know not
I transcend, I migrate, to another, but predict I cannot;

Sometimes I feel, I am like a rolling stone
at the mercy of the body, I am to adorn
whose deeds, the karmas, which decide it all
I languish in this cycle, humbled, I feel small;

Some say I am unique, some say I am one with the Lord
some say I am afloat, ever yearning to seek God
some say I am the core, the centre, integrating one and all
I shudder, I tremble, I know not my own self, the least of all;

I am but confused, many a time
who is me, I or my attire, so fine
I do get attached, to this me of mine
yet selfish I am, to walk away when it is time;

Sometimes I sit back and reflect
ever on move, I wonder, if I could select
like all, be back to dust and be done with it all
destined I am to traverse, endless is this journey after all;

There is a way out, tedious and complex, I am told
the route of meditation, by whom, by me, or the one I ensoul
would it lead to salvation, moksha or nirvana, to end this role
I wish I were mere human, but to migrate, I were my own soul.

***

11
The Solitude

In solitude I remain
from the crowds I want to refrain
to emptiness, I withdraw, to collect my thought
away from all, to myself, I choose my own spot;

I shut the windows, peeping in my heart
I block all entries and set up to start
I focus and look inwards
at peace I am with myself;

I close my eyes and probe my mind
I dig deep, for what I wish to find
sometimes when my mind does soar
in a trance I am, the ideas restore;

I often practice, to step in and outside
at will out of my own shell, as I desire
but loneliness keeps knocking at the door
I hang on, lest the intruder, comes to the fore;

What drives me, I am unable to conjure
what inspires me, I have yet to explore
is it my love or the quest from within
or both in unison, so may it seem;

Nonetheless, great phenomenon, this solitude is
allows a tiny thought, to grow to a flowering tree
this is where I recharge my freshness, to say the least
enervated by the fire, unleashed is the energy so released;

The urge persisting but thoughts evading
I continue to fall back and disappear within
to myself I retract, enlightened, I see hope in a ray
I would be different, had solitude not come my way.

***

12
Wings

Watching the tidal waves recede
lost was I in my dreams, on the beach
a treat to the eye, a flock of geese flew by
arrow in formation, soaring high up in the sky;

They appeared to be following the coastal line
whence to whither, I was unable to surmise
appeared they migratory, wandering across the globe
thought provoking their profile, more I wanted to probe;

Majestic were the birds, flapping at ease in flight
gliding in wake of the draft, to their hearts' delight
light body, large wing span, ideal, for a long haul
flight path pre-determined, etched in their heart;

Soon a strange thought flashed within
how would it be, if I too had the wings
at will I would fly, from dale to dale
soar up in the sky, glide down the vale;

Revolutionary be the change, a life I never knew
enthralling would it be, to catch the bird's eye view
to breathe a breath of cool air, fly up the mountain top
or to the meadows in the far distance, fly non stop;

Each day would be new, eager to awake
to cross the ocean, or stop by at a lake
live off the land, no more worries to care
new found liberty, no inhibitions or fear;

I stretch my imagination, why me alone
why not all be winged, flying like a drone
little need for a car, a plane or a tram
easy to hop, rare would be the traffic jam;

Life as usual, only mode of movement, to facilitate
be able to fly across the continents, nothing at stake
no passport, no visa, the travel just a piece of cake
O Lord! even if an experiment, do try, for what it takes.

***

13
The Conflict Within

A constant tussle, ever astir in the thought
conscious or subconscious, who calls the shots
the mind within, or the mind without, I am at a loss
control by the present, or resistance by the past;

Torn between the two
I know not, who controls who
the past, from the deep within
or the present, waiting in the wings;

Is it the fear, to deviate from the trodden path
resist the logic of present, or follow the psyche of the past
to close the chasm, between sub and the conscious to say
to bring these in harmony, I know not how, I just pray;

I think hard, but the rift is deepening
finally I decide to explore, why is this happening
sub and the conscious, are two states of the same mind
I relax and think, why the ripples, answers I am able to find;

The mind is one, the states may be two
the sub stores the memory, this is so true
I must unfetter my mind, from shackles of the past
let the data be in store, to be mined, but not to decide the path;

The mystery unfolds, as I go further in this maze
the brain is rhythmic, pulsating and in many a state
I relax and dream in one, active in another one, to float
yet a state in between, to create, where I draw from both;

In gratitude I stand, thanking the Lord, unabated
this wonderful phenomenon, nature has so created
one storing the memory, without cluttering the mind
in harmony they are, it is for me, what to choose and find.

***

14

At The Cross Roads I Stand

At the cross roads I stand
perplexed, unable to understand
what had and what is happening to me
why this turmoil within, who holds the key;

Is it fame or glory, that I look for
is it the yearning for my love, afar
weird I feel, I can sense the chill
wavering mind, can hardly stand still;

Why am I losing my peace, I know not
why do I keep digging deep down, in my past
why am I unable to focus and move ahead
why this misery, where is the happiness, instead;

When did I last smile, I am unable to recollect
anguish writ within, in façade it does not reflect
have the good days gone for good, sometimes I think
hoping these will return, and retract me from the brink;

I introspect, am I no longer the same that I was
where is my focus, the fire within, as in the past
where is my compassion, why this creeping insensitivity
unable to conjure, I reflect, how to face it all, with dignity;

I struggle within, with none am able to share
at the cross roads I stand, blank in my stare
I see heavy mist, engulfing the roads ahead
unable am I to decide, the direction instead;

A ray of hope does flicker in my mind
the fog will clear and usher in old times
wisdom will dawn, help me understand
until then, at the cross roads I stand.

***

15
The Prison

The prison conjures a feeling so weird
freedom lost, reputation is smeared
the inmates myriad, waiting for their turn
for the hearing, the verdict and some in adjourn;

Some convicted, some in transit, some implicated
some hard core, some victimized, some instigated
some serving long, some just in, some on death row
but confined they are, freedom lost, time dragging, so slow;

High walls, low ceilings, small cells, very little space
sirens blaring, lights glaring, stifling is the place
the fencings, barriers, guards, clinking chains, say it all
resigned to the fate, what else but wait, life is on a crawl;

Strange is a prison, correction facility, it is called
change in attitude to instill, to rehabilitate and reinstall
time to learn, to read, to think and pray for the sunshine
facilities many, but only on paper, inmates taint the mind;

The stigma is worse than the punishment per se
even after time, indelible is the mark, to stay
only when lost, one realizes the value of freedom
fresh air, sunshine, the moon, the stars, only for some;

A strange thought crosses my mind, to state
from the prison of concrete, one may escape
there is yet a virtual prison, worse than hell
the prison within, confining us to our own cell;

None the better, we all are prisoners of sorts
I too am my own prisoner, to say the least
I build walls around, to solitude I retreat
imprisoned I am to my conscience and my thoughts
to my love, my ideas, to my present and my past;

As I stretch my imagination, to think of my soul
permanent it may be, but its freedom too is on hold
imprisoned it is in my body, it has so leased
it too is serving its time, till it is due for release.

***

16
The Walls

Walls and walls, I see them all around
supporting ceilings, buildings they surround
giving shape, delineating, creating niches, so many
barricading, inducing perception of privacy, security if any;

Myriad is the variety, sleek are the walls
there is much more, just brick and mortar, is not all
prefab, concrete block, cinder, sandstone and many more
aesthetics pleasing, frameless, glazed, colourful glass, encore;

Transparent to some, blocking the view to many
shining, reflecting, engulfed by, ultra cacophony
high rise, low rise, retaining, infrastructure they support
experts mushroom, grand is the décor, within and without;

But these are not the only walls, that I seek and pry
there are yet tougher, not visible, to the naked eye
these are the walls, we build, day in and day out
in compartments we remain, within our clout;

Walls of psyche, the barriers, hard to penetrate
like in a black hole trapped, nothing does escape
agonizing is this misery, of our own creation
ego, arrogance, whatever, leading to frustration;

Sometimes I wonder, this wonder of a wall
simple in concept, the idea keeps stretching across
individuals, states, nations, all busy building the walls
eager to possess, assert, encroach, isolate, block them all;

Physical walls are welcome, but the mental to spurn
let people transcend the barriers of the heart, life be fun
let the partitions be transparent, enabled to see through
let the hearts and souls unite, love permeate, the world to woo;

I sit and muse with my back to the wall
could there be a world, with no walls at all
porous be the lines, free to traverse across
united be the planet, peace for ever to last.

***

17

This Much and No More

Spic and span, well lit was the place
looked efficient, one could draw some solace
the pain though painful, but mitigation too, in the air
mixed were the reactions, some in pain, some in prayer;

Worried look on the faces, myriad was their need
some diagnosed, some yet to be, all anxious indeed
some in the process, complex may be their case
simple tests if indifferent, yet higher to take place;

Varied tests, scans, neuro, cardio, external and incisive
much awaited were the results, as life depended on these
anxiety writ large, some dreaded ailment be symptomatic
life would never be the same thence, only hope for reprieve;

I sat there waiting, friend in coma, at peace, the wards in frenzy
would he or wouldn't he make it, when and how, all so hazy
docs hopeful but non-committal, would the recovery swing
on life support, miserable, yet to life, one yearns to cling;

Transit camp of life it was as if, gave me the impression
some coming alive, some parting from it, some in transition
looked too good to be true, costs or more, not much the frown
covered or not, though eye fixed on the cap, to meet the crown;

But this one was only for some, not the one for one and all
the people at large hardly dare to enter such a place, if at all
theirs is a different world, the place for them, ever crowded
queues, patients sprawled on the floor, waiting, docs hounded
some moving with drips in hand, some with nowhere else to go
neither the cover, nor the funds, at mercy of the fate, to say so;

I reflect, could one draw a line, how much should one endure
ethics, tradition, emotions, law, responsibility, all to the fore
to be selfish to usurp the effort and all the resources, for sure
who can decide but the person himself, this much and no more.

***

18

Those Dirty Hands

Stranded was I enroute
in my ride, some trouble did shoot
the area lonely, route out of way
no traffic, much was there to scare

The sun receding, dusk setting
darkness, threatening to descend,
desperate was I, till I chanced upon
a wayside garage, as if a Godsend;

Confident was the hand
quickly did he make me mobile
disarmed was I, by their attention
and reach out, all this while;

To add, they declined even the costs
a generous gesture, sure it was
gratified, I shook hands with one and all
promised to return and sped off;

I all but forgot the episode, until
a smear of grease, I did notice on my sleeve
flashed back the episode, the warmth to feel
the affections, this smear I wanted to keep;

Unassuming was the young hand
but dexterity and skill par excellence
the rest of the crew too, eager, helpful
they exuded an air of confidence;

Soon a feeling engulfed me
so much more, to reflect
the innovative mind
to undertake the challenge
with little training to help;

Attitude so positive
generous and not extortive
rare to find, in all this glitter
but not uncommon, in our interiors
a true reflection of our culture;

So much to learn from,
this bunch of innocent minds
who appear so simple
but display traits, rare to find;

Humbling was their thought
imprint on my mind, so grand
how pure, were their hearts
though dirty were their hands.

***

19

Am I A Stranger

Strange feelings, I get many a time
that I am a stranger, well past my prime
strange appears this world, so well I have known
I was here only yesterday, but am no longer the one;

Immersed in my thoughts, I often think
is this my world, my very own, why this de-link
the world in which I reveled, excelled and exalted in delight
why this sudden estrangement, hollowness, I shudder with fright;

Life has given me so much and much more to ask
why this feeling, was it simmering, am unable to grasp
why this emptiness, engulfing, blanking my thought
stranger even from myself, this life, I so fondly had sought;

Is it for love, or loneliness by design, for my solitude
unable to surmise, dazed am I, peace decides to elude
why unfamiliar in the territory, so well known in the past
what has estranged, me myself, my will, or the link, I ask;

Alarmed am I, will this state be permanent to sustain
or just a passing cloud, whiff away, with no trace of pain
whatever it be, a stranger is an outsider, it set me thinking
a boon or a bane to be an outsider, myriad thoughts surging;

Strange are the ways of this world, to recall
I close my eyes, past moments, I remember them all
moments of passion, of love, of joy or otherwise
sad, if I be deprived of this link, vital, as elixir for life;

Bewildered am I, this transition, in my heart and my soul
feeling of own creation or imposed beyond my control
a feeling of detachment, to sever from misery of the past
to unshackle, unload, unburden and get on without a stop;

A strange thought flashes across, as I reflect
could I be an enigma, my mind not easy to detect
be an outsider, retain the past, yet control window to the heart
savour what I wish to and be estranged from the rest of my past.

***

20
The Tenant

Polite was his demeanour, smart and elegant
impressed was my friend, to meet his new tenant
suave, polished, humble, correct, was his behaviour
decent were the terms of lease, goodwill in the air;

The relationship flourished, in time the tenant chose to wed
mutual regards in place, communications frank, nothing unsaid
time flew by, soon the lease fell due, to renew or terminate
my friend was polite, but the tenant less inclined to vacate;

Time kept ticking, their warmth soon was ebbing
my friend needed the place, but bonhomie was missing
polite messages were declined, feelings but verged on hate
the suave tenant, regular in payment, but reluctant to vacate;

Soon the rift grew, from minor to a big cleft
pleasantries absent, peace of mind too, as if had left
vacate at any cost, actions now legal, not in a haste
contact now via the court, but the tenant won't vacate;

Years passed by, my friend had aged and so had the tenant
life so peaceful, unwittingly overtaken, by the wretched events
legal issues became a habit, an occupation full time, to state
attitudes hardened, one to evict, the other not to vacate;

What an irony of fate, total life, ill spent
a small issue, but the ego, both refusing to relent
the issue became the raison d'etre of life, for both
gain hardly any, but the loss colossal, had taken its toll;

Sometimes I hope, there be a turn and good sense may prevail
the owner could, the tenant too, alternate options, could avail
my friend could accept him as a friend, son or whatever
how true the adage, if you can't fight, join them with pleasure;

In reflection I wonder, how the events unfold in life
an innocuous issue blown up, so much was the hype
lest we forget, we too are but tenants in this world to state
the soul has leased the body, ever on a short notice, to vacate.

***

21

Seeing Is Believing

Seeing is believing, that's what they say
belief keeps one going, if faith stays that way
love at the first sight and much more to find
all this, the act of seeing, or else one is blind;

Act of seeing, is also the visual perception
wonderful gift, to view the cosmic reflection
to view the glory of the sun, in its crimson splash
soothing silver of the moon, the stars twinkle in their bash;

To savour, the bounty of the lush green meadows
myriad hues dotting the valleys, amazing is nature's show
saplings, the plants, the flowers, the tall trees in sway
what a blessing, for my eyes to see, what they may;

To view thy creation, thy people big and small
innocence of a child, full of life, in its toddle and fall
what a sight it is for me to see my love who I want to see
riot of colours, larger than life, is this ocular faculty;

Simple is this sensation, synonymous with life
yet so complex a phenomenon, not easy to describe
the lens, the pupil, allowing just the correct light, through
eyes and the nerves in harmony, recreating the image so true;

Retina, the screen, where the image is so formed
vitreous gel, to fill the space, the eye ball and around
complex is the neural network, triggered by the sensory cells
master mind, the brain, perfects the image, presented so well;

In awe of nature, a strange thought does cross my mind
this complex network, flawless, day and night, unsupervised
to think, if even some tiny part be impaired, beyond correction
I shudder, how would the vision be, long, short, fading or none;

The truth dawns, come time, serious can be the impact
unable to view the bounty of nature, life will be different
left to enjoy the glory of this world, only in imagination
I am in a hurry, I want to read what I can, to see what I can
I want to fill my memory, with the beauty of this creation.

***

22

Am I For Ever

They say, I am for ever
I shine for ever and last for ever,
buried deep in the earth, am deep down to my size
intense heat and pressure, I take for ever, to crystallize;

Strange is my birth, it takes volcanic eruptions, for me to erupt
the magma carries me along, with igneous rocks, I lie flush,
I cool in the alluvial deposits, those who venture, I am their find
an expert eye fishes me from debris, leads me to the grind;

I am no longer free thereafter, a different life is lying in wait
I am a prized possession, priced by my looks and my weight
I am highly specified, many Cs they have coined for me
an expert cutter examines my cleavage, cuts my shapes to be;

Finally I sparkle, refracting light within, reflecting it without
my luster is supreme, dazzling flashes of light, I am all about
though a mere element, but now I am, the crowned jewel
ready to be set in the jewellery, to adorn the most beautiful;

To my final destination, change many hands, hard is the travel
if rare am I, easy am I not to get, until down comes the gavel
though hardest substance known, yet softest spots do I adorn
the cleavage, earlobes, the soft fingers and else, that be known;

I had my patrons in the royalty, queens, princesses, the crown
now the rich and the mighty, they buy me with no frown;
I am the preferred choice, when they exchange the vows
strange I feel, they love me not, but my cost, but who knows;

Some times I reflect within, not the light but my thoughts
how I loved to be in the wilderness, life though not so soft
I could as well be black or grey, if not crystallized
but free I would be, not be enslaved, due to my shape and size;

My flaws and blemishes are for the experts
I hide the same of those who I adorn no less,
but they ever look for more, as they can buy more
I remain in wraps, I think I am not for ever, anymore.

***

23

The Scorching Sun of May

O the scorching sun of the month of May
blazing at thy peak, as if for ever to stay
piercing are thy rays, with vengeance radiating
an adventure to venture out, thy wrath is penetrating;

Have thee reached thy epitome or the worst yet to come
glaring is thy presence, all pervading, O! our mighty Sun
intense thy power, overflowing, roaring as if in angst
writhing are the lesser mortals, by thy fury, in their midst;

But ungrateful we are not, we still pray all the time
thy energy we absorb, the flora and fauna, it is our life line,
thy heat unleashes aqueous deluge, from the glacial snow
triggering the cycle of energy, keeps the life in flow;

Little do we know, constant turmoil thou are in, with no break
thy core ablaze with fusion, plasmatic ball of fire, so to state
thou are our star, a yellow star, hub of the solar presence
burning within yet radiating unabated, we bow in reverence;

Thou have no boundaries, visible edge is thy photosphere
thy corona, expanding, extending, beyond thy atmosphere
splendid sight thee present, end to end, time to time, in eclipse
a diamond ring, hot spots myriad, cyclical, a galactic bliss;

Surely not scorching all the time, when cool, thou are welcome
soothing, warm, splashing resplendence, when not wholesome
we bask in thy glory, travel afar for thy glimpse, or even a tan
deprived of thy power are those at the poles, short is thy span;

I stretch my imagination, to reflect, who is greater, thee or else
thou are fiery, control our cycle of day and night, to bless
scorching thou may be forcing us indoors, but not all
many a humble soul brave thy wrath, yet cool they are.

***

24

When Will It Be June

When you left, I recall your parting words
gone will be I, but not, as if not to be heard
hope to return, when the needful is done
other than me, the happiest will be none;

The decision to depart, you kept close to your heart
I tried in vain, but none could change your thought
was it someone else, your compulsion I could not surmise
I had to but accept with a smile, this unwelcome surprise;

Quiet was my façade, but turmoil within
why and what was your cause, why this drift, set in
saving grace was your whisper, your task may prune
and if all went well, you were to return by June;

Simply said, but June, was a long time hence
what could not be cured, had to be endured thence
all but to wait and keep your memory alive
hoping your separation, I will be able to survive;

Way hence, I wished, faster would roll down the calendar
June came, but neither your message, nor your splendour
time slid by, your memory too, slowly receded
I trudged to new vistas, fresh pastures precipitated;

The flame of love lay buried, deep within residing
on hold as if, new challenges in life, overriding
with time life drifted, new was the direction
nor did one reminisce, till this reflection;

A strange thought did cross my mind
would love persist, if time was to rewind
how would it be, if June it had been
would life be different or monotony crept in;

As if in a dream, I sit back to recollect
to take a stock of life, what I missed, what did I get
I smile, I had a fair deal, nothing more was there to seek
the moments of love even if short, fill life, so they speak.

***

25

In Gratitude I Remain

In gratitude I remain, humbled to all
the list is long, in generosity, they stand tall
grateful I am to Thee, my Master, first of all
transforming me from a mere thought, to a baby, though small;

I owe myself to my parents, for their warmth and affections
yet more to my siblings, for their so protective a protection
in gratitude I bow to my teachers, for shaping my mind
to my friends, their selfless support, with no axe to grind;

Grateful am I, to my colleagues for their tolerance
though competing, they sure are men of substance
grateful am I to my love, it has made me come alive
it spurred me to dream and reach for the sky;

I owe my very being, in turn to my family
wife doting, caring, children even more
the next generation not lagging, ever in smile
pure and innocent, taking life in their stride;

I cannot but, bow to the nature for its wonderful display
to the sun, for its brilliance, the moon for its silvery array
the vales, the meadows, the mountains, the rivers and all
I am grateful to the mighty wind, its power holds me in awe;

The list is long, O Lord, you top it again
allowing me to flourish in my loss and in my gain
so much you have given me, I feel guilty all the time
in ever asking Thee, for strength and peace for my mind;

I am yet grateful to many in misery, may be lesser a soul
my humble offerings, sufficient in part, if not for their whole
disarmed by their warmth and to see them break into a smile
elegant even in pain, deprived, yet ever ready to sacrifice;

And then came the turning point
it changed the way, I had looked at life
I reflect, what had I done, how life had gone by
had I also taken steps, worth leaving a trace
I hardly could count, I am now in a hurry
to catch up, not much time left to waste.

***

26

The Railway Station

I am lost in the mammoth crowd, struggling, jostling
sea of humanity incredible, from nowhere erupting
whistles, hooters, clinking noise, the trains resounding
hustle and bustle, hurry and worry, panic permeating;

I wait in this unending queue, after a hard day's toil
I know I will lose my wage, yet travel I must, to my soil
in this unbridled crowd, I see no hope for an entry to travel
I am hungry, I feel weak, yet hoping something will unravel;

This is a massive junction, a confluence of many directions
the staff busy, aptly handling, the flow beyond imagination
the last minute counters flooded, staff unable to control
they must plan, they say, I would, but I live from day to day;

I look around, I am not alone, there are many like me, abound
last minute releases, payments withheld, jobs lost in each round
wither the luxury of leave or stability, daily wager, that I am
many like me, flood the stations, deprived of the luxury to plan;

The trains are many, yet unable to cope, we too are too many
sure I will get to travel, but general compartment it will be
we will huddle, falling over each other, but never complaining
grateful I am, allowed in, homewards bound, so comforting;

Sometimes I close my eyes, I dream of my life back home
the cool stream, lush green valley, beautiful hills around
fragrant flowers, peace and calm, people helpful and eager
why I had to be away, was it the misery, greed or hunger;

I chose to be away, to earn extra, hoping to be back soon
the reality dawned, it was the go between, who got the boon
saving to send home the most, myself living frugal to the bone
aging before age, I kill my soul and defer my return home;

If I was granted one wish, the wish, my Master, will be so
I seek no comfort, no luxury, I ask, create me must, if ye so
grant me a life of dignity and right to an occasional smile
why shuttle for a wee bit extra, at the cost of my very life.

***

27
It Set Me Thinking

Life was bliss and passing fast
moments flying, time whizzing past
full of thrill and activities galore
how I wanted this to last and much more;

Love, romance, adventure and what all
emotions, sensitivity, stability as if not all
life fairly rewarding, youth still persisting
content and happy, thankful for thy blessing;

A packed routine, filled to the brim
plenty workout, hunger to stay trim
hunger extended, to read more and more
only to learn, how much one did not know before;

Plenty happened and plenty yet to go
so much favour, the life too good to be so
but true it was, to be happy or otherwise
with only a thin line apart, to be on either side;

Sometimes I wondered, what made it all happen
was it my effort alone or blessing from the heaven
as if in a dream, no situation seemed too dull or bright
living from moment to moment, every moment as if my prime;

And then, the mystery demystified, the inevitable came
shaken out of my reverie, persisted an undesirable pain
the pain did disappear, but not without leaving its mark
it set me thinking, not as it be, it was a matter of heart;

Persuaded, with reluctance, I went to see the doc
the impact there be on my life style, round the clock
lo behold, he did give me a preliminary shock
then he smiled and cleared me on the spot;

Those were the longest moments, of my life
the doc serious and taking time, to decide
once over the hump, plenty crossed my mind
how my life be, if it was to be otherwise;

It set me thinking, O Lord, ye have thy ways
to keep us, the lesser mortals, in our place
none can think big and get away for free
you keep the strings and pull them at will.

***

28

First Shower of Monsoon

Much awaited, are thou
much loved, are thou
what a relief, bring thou
the first shower of the monsoon;

Like a child, I look at the sky
is it overcast, or otherwise
are the clouds heavy, or light in nature
will they loosen, strings of the moisture;

What a specter, thee transcend
the hills afar look hazy, in thy trend
the trees closer, are awash by thy stare
the ambience, as if bathed afresh, none to spare;

I watch droplets, of thy stream
trickle down, my windscreen
some hanging on, tiny pearls, they seem
enthralling is their rhythm, on the scene;

I watch the lovers, step out
walking hand in hand, many sprout
in the park, the pathway has come alive
to relish thy splendour, all as if, on a high;

I watch the maidens, frolic in the street
bright in dress, demure, dreamy, so to speak
the umbrellas too, are colorful in the open
thy arrival, has transformed the horizon;

I too love to be out, in thy domain
unmindful of the drizzle I remain
I am lost in a reverie in thy stream
I think of my love, as if in a dream;

If I may, a plea does cross my mind
maintain the romance in the air, be mild
recharge us deep with water, our life line
why unleash thy fury, for no reason and rhyme.

***

29

The Moments I Love to Live

I have lived as if, for ages afore
I have lived moments galore
moments both dull and bright
but real moments, not in sight;

I have lived a wonderful life
memorable present and the past
time spent well, the strides were fast
but moments worthy, I hardly recall;

Merely to live, is it the life, I wonder
is a busy life only, be life's plunder
event to event, with no time to stop by
is it living or evading, whom and why;

I have had my moments of thrill, besides
spurring my thoughts to excel and thrive
moment in love, moments in pleasure and pain
relished every moment, be it in loss or in gain;

The past was good, with nostalgia they say
but the present is to live, the future, still in fray
hollowness, sometimes creeps in my thought
time spent in futility of this life, I am distraught;

What must I do, to keep my mind still
thoughts and deeds, that give me thrill
have I just wasted away, my long years
have I lost out on the sunshine, I fear;

I close my eyes and recall, many a moment of past
with my love, hoping for ever, the moments to last
a walk in the rain, rhythmic in its fall, would it be
splash of the mountain stream, soothing it was to me;

Let the moments linger, in my thought and deed
let purity of my compassion, transcend for all in need
to be ever in love, pure, innocent and selfless, may I be
content and happy in these moments, that I love to live.

***

30

That Streak of Grey

Charged with bundles of energy and dressed to kill
I saw my reflection, in disbelief, I just stood still
the mirror had captured it all, it sure had a tale to tell
a streak of grey hair pronounced, mocking back at will;

Greying! Started already, how could it be true
had life slipped by so much, seemed so untrue
had I drifted away, or had I steered my way through
was my youth to last only that much, if it was to be true;

That single streak of grey, was thought provoking
wonderful moments of my past started flocking
past, thrilling it was, the challenges faced, in a stride
so early! I thought in dismay, set to recede, the spice from life;

A look at my image and yet another thought flashed
was it a gate-crasher or a harbinger for many more, to splash
greying had to happen sooner or later, but natural in this race
whatever it be, it lent dignity to aging, to grow old with grace;

Unable to reconcile, many a thought crossed my mind
I hardly had started and here I was, edging past my prime
was it to be the beginning of the end, or end of the beginning
what about my love, my aspirations, I was falling short of time;

Was this streak acting on my psyche, my thoughts, or my deed
hide I can the one external, but how to hide the one, within
I have unfinished business plenty, I wonder, would I last a while
would I be able to finish my chores, or be done in the last mile;

I wonder if I am brooding, or thinking much, about the change
would this change usher in a new era, or my life to rearrange
those compliments, admiring looks, no longer, life so strange
all this until nature stepped in, and this stress and strain;

With time I realise, nothing has changed, I am the same, within
why fret, when the frame is still robust and the heart vibrating
why worry now, the countdown started, with my first breath in
I decide, to be as before, live the life my way and not give in.

***

31
Reminiscences

Ere I realized, I was past my prime
unable to comprehend, how flew the time
the way it has, it must have passed well
the pace fast, ever on run, but nothing rings a bell;

Then came the turn around, I peeped into my past
memories started surfacing, from the depth of my heart
some pleasant, some not so, but a message they had brought
my aspirations, dreams, of what one got and what one had lost;

The time spent with nature, I loved to stretch
in the mountains, the ambience so pure and fresh
the mountain stream, splashing, rhythmic in flow
watching it curl down, in its own high and low;

I recall, fragrance of the daffodils
inhaling, absorbing, to my heart's fill
the meadows and the clouds rising
romance in the air, love thriving;

One was, as if ever in love, with the love besides
only if it could stand still, time only would decide
how would it be, nature had some other designs
the pain too was waiting, as a part of this rhyme;

And then one had to leave and depart
for greener pastures, to play my part
in a new world, the challenge apart
would I be fine, or be distraught;

Now that the time has gone by, I think but resist
should I recall and relive, what all one has missed
in anguish I see, the worth of all that has gone by
why turn the clock to relive, what I could not live by;

I step out, of the time machine
I recollect all, that life has been
what all I got and what all have I not
futility of this cycle of present and my past.

***

32
Where Were You

Where were you, when I was down and under
where were you, when I was up and about
where were you, in my rise and in my fall
was I for you, or you for me, if at all

I looked for you, beyond the yonder
dreaming of you, even in my slumber
seeking you, in my heart and my soul
but you, evading, taking my toll;

Knew ye not, my love was ever thine
knew ye not, of this feeling divine
knew ye not, the pangs it would create
but in love, I am resigned to my fate;

Sometimes I feel, you seek my devotion
sometimes I feel, you sense my passion
my thoughts, revolve around you, my love
what else, if this be not, my confession;

I remain amused, by this ever illusive phenomenon
my thoughts fleeting, my mind ever on the run
is my love for my love or a fancy of my own creation
I allow my love to flourish, it fills me with elation;

I now can see, where were you, all this time
you were ever here, amused, in this dilemma of mine
peeping in my heart, watching intently, screening
rekindling the fire, giving my life a whole new meaning.

***

33

I Live in My Shadow

Taking myriad shapes, with my every stance
in the wake of light, or in its fleeting glance
from long to short, from leading to lagging
my shadow, inseparable from me, hugging;

Sometimes swamped, by yet longer shadows
of the swaying trees, some fast, some slow
overwhelmed by their dance, rhythmic in spree
my shadow yearns to be active, in this melee;

Am I my shadow, or the shadow is mine
one dark, the other brilliant, in its shine
which one is what, a wonderful combine
who lives in whose shadow, me or mine;

A strange thing I observe, of my shadow
it chooses to hide, when I am in the bright
withdrawing, admiring me a-glow, in the light
ecstatic with love, or thrilled by my very sight;

Is it in love, or it chooses to suffer the pain
elusive to my touch, inexpressive it does remain
hiding, teasing, appearing, appealing, adapting
ecstatic, as if in a trance, the love is ever lasting;

Soft and imperceptible, but never urging
I know not the inspiration, that is surging
fondly following my movements, replicating
me or my shadow, in unison mutually relating;

In a reverie I reflect, only to find, that I am but amused
this intermingling play of hide and seek, I am but confused
yearning for the soft caress, yet will the twain ever meet
my shadow at hand, alluding but haunting me even in my sleep;

Strange is this phenomenon, of thy creation,
ever together, yet persistent is this separation
though virtual, ever willing to lose its being, for me
pure and selfless as my shadow, how I wish, I could also be.

***

34
What Was My Fault

I see the beauty of this world
but from a distance
I relish the luxuries of this world
but from a distance;

I see the illumination and the festivities
but from a distance
I relish aroma of the delicious dish
but from a distance;

I longingly look at the school
I know not, what they teach there
I longingly look at the luxurious apartments
I know not, how they live there;

I happily see, beautiful children go by
smartly dressed, pleasant in their smile
I watch them, in their laugh and fun
but with each other, with me none;

Sometime, I am not well
I keep it to myself
I have many siblings
we have nothing to share;

I see my mother go off to work
to clean these luxurious dwellings
sometimes, she takes me along
I can sense, what be in the offing;

Sometimes, I foolishly dream
I dream of going to school
I dream to also look pretty
I dream also to relish the life
in real life and not from a distance;

I hear, I have added to the population
that I am, a burden on civilisation
in agony, I ask thee, my creator
I never asked thee
why did thee create me
what was my fault?

***

Section – II
Someone Somewhere

35

Someone Somewhere

I know, you are there somewhere
I know there is someone, for whom I care
there is a heart that beats for me, I am aware
my heart too yearns, for someone somewhere;

How I long, for a glimpse of thine
how I dream, of your form sublime
how I think, of you all the time
my quest continues, for my love divine;

How I long, for a touch of thine
how I have wandered, into many a shrine
how I love you, to be a shadow of mine
my quest remains, but you are hard to find;

Are you a myth, a mystery or mystique
are you for real, in flesh and blood, so to speak
are you near or far, or hiding behind a veil
you torment me, unable to find, you leave no trail;

I live with your memory, since the times I recall
you are an image, etched deep in my heart
bathed in the glow of the morning sunshine
eagerly I await to be with you, O love of mine;

Is it love, devotion or else, I am not aware
transformed am I, by the love and compassion, so rare
I close my eyes, hoping you to be there, in my stare
your image remains elusive, though I seek every where;

Sometimes I reflect, is my love blind, what else
is it rational, from thin air, so much to expect
but my heart and soul are one, for you they crave
I continue my quest, I know you are there, somewhere.

***

36

Freedom

They say, we have earned our freedom
freedom of thought, speech and action
they say, our country is free
free they are and so are we;

I am amused, I reflect
am I really free
can I do, what I want to do
can I live, the way I want to;

The fetters, are many
at every step, is tyranny
bonded am I, by rules and the law
liberated though, but there is some flaw;

Creativity urges my mind to float
free like a bird, unhindered it should soar
but fettered I remain, in heart and my soul
surrendered to my love, my freedom is on hold;

Many more, yet wait with the chains
social, religious, traditions, to name
deeper I sink in this quagmire, I try in vain
freedom in name, but bonded I remain;

As I look around, I am not alone
many in misery, deep to the bone
live like animals, basic needs hardly met
I am ashamed, free them from poverty, be our debt;

One strange thought, dares to flash across
let fetters be external, but free be my heart
as I look inwards, it is a matter to be distraught
the worst is internal, I am captive even to my thought.

***

37

The Hand Bag

Time was flying, life wonderful as could be
had ample and more, grateful I was to Thee
if there was an offer, to ask for yet more
at a loss would I have been, unable to conjure;

Contented at heart, sound was the sleep
until a dream, that changed my life in a beep
The Lord offered me a strange dispensation
a hand bag I could carry, was his consideration
to carry in my journey last, on to the world beyond;

Thrilled was I, with the Lord's grace
this was special, with none I could share
I set about to plan, very methodically
what all I should pack, with me to carry;

The list I drew, started to grow longer
until, the self prevailed and came out stronger
after much deliberations and a serious thought
I finalized the list, to keep within the size I got;

First and foremost, figured the memories of my past
some photographs to reminisce, all etched in my heart
some letters of love, that I had read and re-read a lot
my favourite songs, stored, transporting me to my past;

Some more, the books I liked, these were like friends
paper and pen, to complete my next book, depends
I also packed my favourite golf balls, that go far
finally my whisky glass, just in case, there be a bar;

Closer the time, eagerly I checked with the undertaker
how would the bag go, on person or in the cargo
soon I was to realize, on person, it could not be
it had to be booked, assigned to the next world, for me;

The undertaker had seen life, this proposal he won't bite
seeing the impasse, I was in dilemma, finale not so bright
then broke my sleep, I woke up to realize, all this was a dream
I smiled, the Lord had a message for me, as it would seem
meager are real needs, revelation it was, though in a dream.

***

38

If I Had a Choice

If I had a choice
many a thought, would surge in me
first would it be, to be, or not to be
if yes, the next, what or who to be;

If I still had a choice
I would seek, all there is to be
to rise in life, the top it should be
to be in the forefront, in whatever I did;

If all above was granted
thoughts about myself, there would be
the attitude in life, what it should be
open, exclusive or indifferent it be;

If the option to opt still persisted
I would think, should love in my life be
my love be mad, blind, or planned it be
surrender in love, or to surrender love, if need be;

If I had a choice, how my heart be
memories in store, compassion there be
self centered in thought, for myself only
or pure and transparent, like a child it be;

If I had a choice, how my eyes to be
full of dreams and a glint in these be
expressive, bold, look straight in the eye, to be
or evasive, thoughtful, cold in stare, these be;

I sit back and reflect, how in life, it all has been
choicest of the choices met, what more there be
am I happy and content, with all the needs that be
strange, I find peace of mind evading, anguish lurking indeed;

Selfish I have been, all my thought, for none other than me
if I had yet one more choice, pray undo all, that I got for free
late to realize but firm in resolve, to think of others, in need
I start afresh, renewed in vigour, chastised, but happy indeed.

***

39

Poetry

Emerging from dreams, some random thoughts
love, romance, emotions, sensibilities besought
stretching the imagination, beyond the horizon
aesthetic it is, literary marvel, past comparison;

Weaving in observations, experiences of life
picking up threads scattered, past comes alive
threading these together, stringing in style
play with the words, sometimes in rhyme;

A literary saga, nurtured by many a heart
alternate expression, evokes emotive response
myriad are its forms, styles, ballads, sonnets and more
absorbing are its rhythm, rhyme and the metaphor;

Reminiscing the past, retracing the love that was
musings in thought, the matter close to every heart
the moments of life, the stress and the strain
takes a stock of life, its loss and the gain;

Love and romance, a poet's delight
the moments spent, with the love beside
moments of separation, the pleasure and its pain
captured beautifully, embedded in heart, these remain;

I too have dared, to dabble in this poetic domain
allowed myself to dig deep within, but in vain
many a thought, often crisscross my mind
am unable to sift, these remain entwined;

Relentless I am still, in my pursuit of this mirage
hoping one day I too, will get a glimpse of this visage
some beautiful thoughts, I also might be able to dream
someday I too may pen, semblance at least, if not a poem.

***

40

I Thought I Had the Courage

I thought I had the courage, to write it all
about sensitivities, events, big and small
I thought I was bold, to be free and frank
the conflict within, withholds my hand;

The reason to withhold, I know not why
who do I shield, what do I hide, why am I shy
do I have some skeletons within, from myself I seek
why this reluctance, why this inhibition, to speak;

I was bold and with courage of conviction
could call a spade a spade, sans inhibition
for my own self, as if a black hole, resides in my heart
unable to tear away from it, leaves me but distraught;

I thought I was open like a book and forthright
why do I withhold my feelings, why now uptight
am I scared, apprehensive or cautious, to say it all
trivial it may be, but uncertain, in some eyes I may fall;

The dilemma keeps lurking, under my stare
I keep it in wraps, deep within, unable to bare
I burn within, yet in façade, happy do I appear
to maintain a balance and stability, in my sphere;

How long I have to live, with a lid on my heart
how long will it take, for me to trigger the start
how long will it take, to speak the truth and face it all
sooner the better, lest the pressure be and no safety valve;

As time goes by, I sit back and reflect
why should I go public, why not deflect
why need to open up, none other is hurt, but I
I decide, simmer within, but keep the smile.

***

41

And Then She Blinked

I wondered, if she was gone for good
in person, but in thoughts, she ever stood
ebbing hope too, had started to slide
it took time, for the feeling to revive;

Love they say, is to surrender, to the sublime
possessive not, selfless it is, follows down the line
time in separation, a meditation, one is inspired to be
heart and soul unite, soar unhindered, as if set free;

Life smooth, moving at its pace, soon came to a halt
at the cross roads we stood, it was time to depart
love transited, visible to invisible, resigned to its fate
desires gone, but feeling of love, never did abate;

With time, love did subside, simmering thoughts yet alive
reveling in thy thought, hoping, the fire was equally alike
soon the mind shut the past, to look at life afresh
plenty more in life than faded memories, a cause of stress;

Strange is life, estranged like strangers, we became with time
chance meetings drew cold stares, blank, bereft of past shine
was it true or were we sitting on a volcano, now overdue
waiting for some trigger, to unleash the deluge;

One fine day appeared she, from nowhere, face to face
was it by chance or design, dazed was I, by her grace
so much had happened, so much lost and now this jinx
dignified she stood, took a deep breath and then she blinked;

I reflect, that blink, so expressive, said nothing, but said it all
she came, she saw, though distant, yet dignified in withdrawal
the past flashed, the blink had rekindled, the dwindled thought
refreshed, recharged, I fondly store that blink, deep in my heart.

***

42

Those Stolen Moments

Those stolen moments I love to relive
to be with my love, whatever life may give
in person or in thought, to be with thee
in these very moments, my mind is set free;

Those stolen moments fleeting, time ever slipping
only if time could stand still, a wishful thinking
I come alive, intoxicated by thy fragrant presence
thy absence ever lurking, I live just in fragments;

Fearing, each such moment may be the last
continuing to shudder, at the very thought
would thee be with me, or transit to my past
reflexively I store thy memory, deep in my heart;

Why do these moments have to be short and stolen
stolen from whom, from me or life, a mere reflection
is my love ephemeral, or forever will it change my life
would the freshness remain and that glint in the eye;

Strange thoughts, do cross my mind, betimes
are these moments for me, or my love sublime
for my heart and soul, to allay the lurking doubts
closing doors to my mind, I let the inner springs sprout;

The moments though stolen, are these for me alone
these are very precious, very private, my very own
spurring my mind, to soar beyond the horizons known
stretching the imagination I recall, how our love has grown;

I reflect in anguish, the guilt to steal
for whom and why, each moment I feel
if for love, let this love be divine
revel in surrender, such love be mine;

I seek, thy indulgence divine
pure and innocent, such love be mine
make my love, as dignified for thee
let the stolen moments, lead me to thee.

***

43

Could It Happen

I was by the river side, music soothing beside
the moon majestic, its rays dancing aside
the stars shining, ambience too, as if the same
hoping, but never expecting and then you just came;

Amused by the patter of the rain
my heart yearned for you, as if in pain
lonely I felt, my heart too, feeling the same
then it happened, first your fragrance and then you came;

The mood was festive, celebrations in the air
all bedecked, immersed in their rejoice and the glare
I was there yet not there, as if present only in name
suddenly I came alive, as from nowhere, you just came;

How did it happen, coincidence, telepathy, I know not
how did our hearts relate, was it merely a thought
whatever the means be, the inspiration was nothing but love
the fire burning alike, the moments, still linger in my heart;

Sometimes I wonder, have you given me a go by
you are there somewhere, how I wish, you be by my side
in hope I remain, I believe, the miracles are not in mere name
could it happen, you walk in softly and surprise me yet again.

***

44
The Siblings

I fondly recall, early years of my past
parents, siblings, the world was small
love and warmth, flowing to the brim
impregnable was the bond, firm within;

Full siblings were we, if not, yet be equally true
pure was love, it only strengthened, as we grew
hierarchy well established, the birth order respected
natural were we, the elders doted, young ones connected;

We had all the fun, but held our values high
whatever be our share, accepted with a smile
hardly missed, what did not come our way
in each other's company, we loved to stay;

The parents loving, helped us in our need
rarely interfering, yet available indeed
we learnt to share, without hesitation
mutually we were, a source of inspiration;

As we grew up, we drifted away from our nest
distances but physical, feelings remained intact
we looked for excuses, to congregate back home
time was never enough, well used was the phone;

With time, imperceptible was the tide
tolerance ebbing, differences on the rise
priorities changing, affections fading
warmth in the relations, as if receding;

And then, the final nail in the coffin
the parents were gone, time for decision
ironic, value of the birth order alluding
urge to usurp others' share, was amazing;

Now that life has gone by, the mist is rising
hard to imagine, same siblings, now conniving
when young, ever ready to forgo, own piece of cake
and now, to snatch from others, one did not hesitate;

How could one be so, for a paltry piece of land
wither the promise, to hold each others' hand
in shame I regret, every moment of my thought
when I crossed the threshold, for whatever I sought
only to realize, so little I gained but so much I lost.

***

45

The Snow Flakes

Tiny snow flakes, brushing past my face
touch of a feather, imperceptible is thy pace
tender and soft, like petals thee are fragile
descending from heavens, dressed in all white;

What a pretty sight, ye the snow flakes, make
appear thee suddenly, unobtrusive in space
thy random drift, a visual feast to watch
a blanket of white, unfurled by thy fall;

Crystalline ice are thee, in clouds thee precipitate
liquid within, frozen outside are thou, our snow flakes
lattice in structure, powdery, when thou fall on ground
cyclic in melt and refreeze, to snow pack thee transform;

If precipitation is unabated, uninterrupted is thy fall
with wind, the snow pack drifts and gathers moss
in thy fumble and tumble, thou grow massive in size
thy powdery roll if triggered, as avalanche thee rise;

If lie frozen for long, thou transform to a glacier
as summer approaches, to thaw and melt thee prepare
thou set off emerald green rivulets from thy snows
as the glaciers melt, rivers recharge us in their flow;

But thou are not mere crystals, we love thee for our fun
fascinating thou are, refreshing us, by thy gay abandon
the snowman, the pellets we love to hurl in thy splash
we sled, we ski, we revel, we build a bonfire, have a bash;

Sometimes, thy life is too short
as thou fall, thou melt or sublimate
but when thou survive and live long
thou go on to be gigantic and strong;

As I reflect, I admire thee, our snow flakes
so tiny, but what a difference to us thou make
selfless in transition, thy identity thou hardly retain
thou are the source, the balance of energy, thee maintain
but for thee, life will be grim, I bow to thee, O our snow flakes.

***

46

O Ye Setting Sun

O ye setting sun! what an imposing spectacle thee present
crimson red hues, reflecting, refracting, in the distance
playing hide and seek, with twilight and dusk in anticipation
the night waiting in the wings, to usher in the transition;

Spectacle out of the world, conjures a feeling of romance
lovers revel in thy charm, huddled, observing thee, in a trance
enthralling are thy colours, mystic thou may seem
generous thou remain, though nearing end of the scene;

It ever is a hard day's work, for thee
with all that heat and turbulence, within
burning within, yet radiating without inhibition
the cost, only thou will know, O our great Sun;

Blessed by thy brilliance and light, splashed besides
we rise to yet another day, fired with a new hope in life
hope for future, to keep us fresh and going, O great Sun
thy setting sets us back, surfaces a weird feeling, within;

I wonder where thou go, after thou call it a day
sliding thy majestic ball of fire, out of this fray
do thou go to sleep, or to light up someone else's life
we wait for thy return, but dread, if it was not to be;

Thou have many such planets, earth is but one
spinning and revolving around thee, ever on the run
just to get their share of glimpse, of thy glow
the life line of energy for all, I wonder if ye know;

Strange thoughts do cross my mind, O our great Sun
myriad forces unleashed in thy absence, hard to imagine
forces of nature, of power, of crime and many such more
victims are the weak, the poor and those unable to conjure;

The misery in thy absence, will set thou afire
if thou were aware, I wonder, would thou ever retire
but retire thou must, for the balance to maintain
for us and the planet, though on fire thee ever remain.

***

47

The Queue

Ever since I recall, barring times a few
merely to survive, I was always in a queue
trapped in this quagmire, I remain in wait
anxious within, the movement, at snail's pace;

Threatened, I have felt all the time
if I didn't go past the line, would all be fine
control I have none, on these queues of mine
what if, this thought, ever weighs on my mind;

The queues, long winding and serpentine
as if ordained to wait, am I, for turn of mine
anxiety lurking, would I make it or otherwise
head of the queue so distant, I struggle to survive;

Sometimes I look around, not all are in the queue
some with a silver spoon, their world! I have no clue
their needs are different, they don't live on the margins
different is their canvas, bigger picture on their horizon;

Life has now gone by, I sit back and reflect
what if, I was not in a queue, how would I react
would my mind also soar, would I also dream
would I also think, would my eyes also gleam;

To be in the queues, was an experience in time
the queue has its own charm, the least, I find
to rub shoulder with all, get a first hand view
I am not alone, many more too, are in the queue;

A strange thought flashes across my mind
in this journey of life, as we near the end of time
those who were in luxury, would they take a view
be in line, or here too, would they jump the queue?

***

48

Adolescence Recalled

Into adolescence, I recall my transition
stepping into adulthood, what a transformation
aware not of the floodgates, to unleash the deluge
swamping my life, the metamorphosis triggered, was huge;

Weird changes, biological, physiological, psychological galore
croaking voice, uneven growth, hair, pimples appearing afore
apparel ill fitting, confidence slipping, depression, looming
strange, why can't the growth be simple and unassuming;

Imperceptible changes in behaviour, in attitude, creeping
peer group pressures, urge for the unknown, persuading
feeling of isolation, self-created complex, simmering
the changes phenomenal, no words of sympathy arising;

Yet more, hormonal releases, sexual changes, precipitating
need for close friends, anxiety to share thoughts, surging
urge to look better, be recognized and shine, dwelling
emotive feelings, romance, desire to love, be loved, swelling;

As I reflect, I feel, adolescence is not all doom and gloom
hope brightening, future inviting, to excel, ample be the room
edge of the horizon and beyond, wonderful the life may seem
to plan and prepare, and take the plunge to fulfill my dreams;

I often fancied adulthood, just around the corner
in transit from the childhood, enjoying also the former
new rights, legal and more, fancy myself to be someone
reveling in the bliss, as if all be bright, and dark side none;

Once past the state of fantasy, it did strike
what actually may be in store, dreams aside
would one take the challenges in a stride
succeed and rise, or fall by the wayside;

I sit back and recall, my adolescence
wonderful were the days, in every sense
youth, bundles of energy, long were the strides
all joy and fun, how I wish I could relive that life.

***

49

The Beard

Many a time a thought did cross my mind
what if, I supported a beard, how would I find
mere change in façade, extended my facial profile be
would only look be different or different at heart, would I be;

Curious I was more, to think of the styles, that be
full, trimmed, side burns, chin strap or goatee, may be
if the moustache be integrated, Hollywoodian it would be
whither my lips, my chin, eyes, I wonder how my smile be;

And then, face to face was an elder, beard full in flow
swaying was the beard, as the wind started to blow
lost was I, gazing at the thick, dense, crop of the strands
hardly could I focus on the face, staring from the other end;

A face, serene, elegant, philosophic, dignified, it was
eyes visible, nose too, lips hardly, hidden was the visage
much that I tried, hardly could I perceive his smile
may be, he exactly knew, what was going on in my mind;

As I probe, beard in flow, was the choice of the men
philosophers, kings, sages and the handsome gentlemen
mandatory for many a cleric, in reverence to the religion
distinguishing the sect, clan, religion, identity for some;

Beards started to disappear, in keeping with the times
restricted to some, the die hard or religious in mind
revolution in trend, may be women too had a hand
tickled in touch and kiss, by the flowing strands;

It was also the time, for me to take a view
would I or won't I, be a bearded man too
I liked the elegance, but I thought for a while
I chose to defer, it was rather late in life.

***

50
Am I Hooked

Glow on the face and glisten in the eye
strange was his excitement, I did not want to pry
beaming with pride, delightful was his look
finally my friend blurted, that he had been hooked;

What a star was he, brilliant and an all rounder
in love and romance, had friends many times over
full of life, bundles of energy, style as if, an open book
would he be the same, time would tell, he is on the hook;

Hooked he was, a slang though, as if he was a fish
would he be suitable too to the palate, as a tasty dish
to fathom a woman's heart, their mate to be good, for good
cherish, possess, love or tease, get him by hook, or by crook;

Knowing his past, to be on the leash, only till, his tether shook
what would be his fate, would he be ever, let off this hook
would he still wander and revert, or play it by the book
old habits die hard, I am curious, but he still is on the hook;

Eclectic are a maiden's thoughts, wandering in all directions
finally coalescing in search of their beau, just an observation
though the dame be pretty, modern and a professional to look
yet eye focused on the finale, to lead her love to the hook;

Traditional hooks are very robust, but flexible to the hilt
sufficient leeway to wander, even ignore, if relented is the guilt
such hooks last life long, easy to guess, it is no wonder
unhooked these are only, when life itself is surrendered;

I was amused, complacent, ignorant, almost indifferent
the plight of my friend, change in his life, so stringent
what he was, and what would he be, ever hereafter
till it dawned, he was not the only one
to walk down the isle, to be on the altar;

Strange thoughts, continued to cross my mind
what would be my response, if I was to be in the bind
in reflection I feel life is a mix, on the hook or otherwise
if pleasure there be in the hook, pain cannot be far behind
all this until, to join the fray, I too had to make up my mind.

***

51

I Am a Dalit

I am a dalit, as called by them all
meaning I learnt, when I grew big and tall
born in a shanty, for ever I lived in one
education some, but pleasures were none;

Strange would I feel, my elders would set off early
what job they had, I was to learn later, but not so happily
return they would, but soiled and seething with smell
was it their sweat of toil, certainly they did not smell well;

We all would huddle together, but not with others
were we different in caste or creed, my mind was a-stir
were we the downtrodden, touchable! or otherwise
I wondered why we were different, I was none the wise;

We lived in dirt, full of dirt, yet more ingrained deep in hands
why so much of dirt, whose, why us, I could hardly understand
we were like all other humans, why us, to be in all this smell
until it dawned, captive we were, designated to live this hell;

I was told, if I studied, glory would come my way
even if mediocre, reservation would hold the sway
I hardly knew the scorn and resentment, would it stir in all
was I selfish, or someone lopsided, robbing Peter to pay Paul;

As I grew up, to schooling indifferent, I followed the elders
to clean and clean and yet more, the soils, but of others
rare would be a chance, or urge to join the main stream
soon I got used to this life, repugnant would it not seem;

I close my eyes and reflect, on why and how of our life
was it the history, the shackles, or the will lacking to strife
many a religion would appease us, and many leaders too
we could sway the balance, large in number and growing so
only some of us could unfetter, the rest remain in status quo;

Sometimes I fancy, have I missed my chances in this very life
to live a life normal like others and not as other caste or tribe
to rise without reservation, to rub shoulders in competition
would it be many generations, magic if sooner, for certain
will the dirt go away by itself, or need to clean will not remain
who will it be, will a new breed surface, but different in name.

***

52

When I Grow Up

When I grow up, I will have many a query to seek
I keep these on hold for now, am too young to speak
enthused by fun and joy, I find life so bright
doting parents, folks back home, too are alike;

Born and brought up was I, in this land of dreams
my parents drifted here, seeking the pastures green
to this land did they migrate, they are the expatriate
their folks, now mine too, still back home, as I state;

The ambience here heavenly, facilities in place
caring teachers, friends eager to help, just in case
many an activity, music, games, painting, the park
I look forward to each day, there is ever a fresh spark;

Often I get a chance, to visit our folks back home
life different, but warmth, affections, wholesome
amazing are the relationships, how they maintain
that is a whole new world, so much time to contain;

As I grow up, the visits back home, too decline
so do the memories, hazy they become, with time
many a question too, keep cropping up in my place
who am I, what ethnicity, the roots, whither my space;

Some times a feeling, does flash across my mind, to say
am I an outsider here, colour of my skin, may come in the way
my ways were different, I have adapted to new life, in a stride
torn am I, between the customs, local and those, I had imbibed;

Although a citizen here, yet they prefix my origin, as Indian
neither Indian, nor non Indian, I am a person of Indian origin
the same am I, the semantics many, why couldn't it be simple
genes are the same, land may differ, with my folks, I resemble;

The time has now gone by, I am on my own, in this strive
reality I must face, I must excel and prove myself, I decide
life is not all gloom, both the worlds, I have tasted to my fill
I am free to pick from both and live the life unto my will
I smile, I keep the links my way, my roots are there to stay.

***

53

When You Were Born

Do you remember
  how tiny were you
    how fragile were you
      when you were born;

Engrossed in your own cycles of milk, ease and sleep
  what were you thinking, to yourself you would keep
    amused as if even in sleep, peaceful was thy smile
      life before and after, or on futility of the cycle of life;

Enchanted was I, by your lovely smile,
  your pink cheeks, kicking sprees and big eyes
    amazing the way, you changed thy resemblance, at will
      till you grew up, to lead thy life, to your heart's fill;

Do you remember, how shy was I
to hold you, to touch you, to kiss you
unable to cope with my status, in elevation
maturing overnight, I was older by a generation;

And then, your travails started
the competition, the pressures
I watched you with concern
but was busy, fighting, my own;

Your struggle to achieve, became ours
your failures and successes, became ours
when you smiled, so did we
when you were hurt, so were we;

Life has gone by, you have risen high
comforting to see, how mature you are
if you are thinking, what I am thinking
you have a tiny one of your own, to care for;

The roles have changed so fast
you are the present, we are the past
we sit on the side lines, waiting
eager to respond, if there is a call.

***

54

The Wind

Whence you come, whither you go
light are your steps, you ever in flow
mighty are you, your power beyond compare
O great wind, with folded hands, I offer my prayer;

Softly you tiptoe, caressing past
you move at will, fearless in trespass
invisible you are, transparent in your quest
evasive to a touch, your presence can just be felt;

When mild, you conjure a feeling of romance
you usher in the fragrance, of my love in advance
I envy, when you brush past my love, in your way
you rekindle the flame, my heart simmers in ache;

You fill our lungs, infusing a fresh breath of life
you strike a melody when you fill my flute inside
you fill the hills, the plains, the valleys, the meadows
endless is your jar, ever filled, generous you are and more;

Sometimes I reflect, what a marvel of nature are you
simple you appear, but complex is your reason to be
pressure and thermal differential, give rise to your flow
no wonder, sometimes you are fast and sometimes slow;

Dull is your mood, when you are calm
eerie silence descends, awaiting thy charm
when gentle breeze you are, romance is in the air
you are welcome at sea, when you rise to be a gale
but ferocious you are, when you become a hurricane;

You ferry the aqueous vapors, gaseous in form
cyclical you are, precipitation of rain you cause
you have been the source of power, for our trade
westerly-easterly combine, round trip would it make;

Your might if harnessed, wonderful will be life
the power so generated, for our needs it will suffice
you are ever in motion, local or coastal, be your flow
you maintain ecological balance, by your motion to and fro;

So much you have done and continue to do
so generous, selfless, yet humble, are you
I envy you, how much I love to be like you;

A strange thought, does flash across my mind
to be free like you and leave my world behind
to ride with you and explore beyond the turn
be rid of my present and past and never to return.

***

55

The Dahlia

As I drew the curtains apart
tip toed, morning sun, sneaking past
brilliant was the golden yellow splash
still half in slumber, I came alive by this flash;

Astonished was I, to see a dahlia peeping in
massive, full in bloom, pink and soothing
swaying lightly with the wind, as if in stupor
like a guest it stood, knocking at the door;

Majestic in its honeycomb, of petals so soft
intricately woven, too delicate, even for a thought
elegant in its posture, it stood exchanging glances
eager to enter, friendly look and so were its advances;

In a trance, I kept admiring this wonder
come evening, it looked down and under
as if robbed of its shine, by the receding sun
was it suffering, in pain of the separation;

Soon it was a-smile, spurred by the lunar splash
it loved to play hide and seek, in the silvery bash
though quiet, but its silhouette, stood firm
alert, as a sentry on the watch, looking stern;

Soon we were friends, I slept in peace, dreaming
safe I felt, I had a friend in my need, waiting
come morning, my friend was a-smile once again
enlivened by the morning sun, relieved of the pain;

Alas! the pleasure of its company, I was to lose soon
harsh fact but true, my friend had outlived its bloom
its life short but memorable, left a lasting trace
dignified, I found my friend, in its poise and grace;

Was it aware, its life spent not in vain
never did it reflect, its anguish or pain
across the barriers, its love did transcend
I wish I be worthy of such a worthy friend.

***

56

The Public Park

Amidst the jungle of concrete, what a refreshing scene
lung space lush green, trees, shrubs and flowers rarely seen
laced with swings, a versatile play wing and a jogger's path
landscaping, arboriculture, planned with a deliberate thought;

Clusters of laburnums flowering in hues rich yellow and golden
the champas, with intoxicating fragrance, one is beholden
bottle brushes huddling, saffron red, the gulmohars flooding
shade loving some, sun loving many, rare is the mix, vibrating;

Pathway, meandering in ecstasy, joggers, jogging
enervated, splurge of health buffs, suddenly surging
fountain snorting rich vaporous splash, up, up and away
nocturnal extravaganza, lights rhythmic, in the gaseous array;

Alloe-Vera proud, cacti in look and succulent grey-green leaf
medicinal in its magic for burns and digestion, instant in relief
lacy asparagus ferns, climbing the exterior, adorning the hem
numerous pixels, fibrous leaves, spread on the flattened stem;

Flowers, enriching the ambience, refreshing heart to the core
dahlias, chrysanthemums, asters, gerbera and many more
rose, the standard, standing tall, cocky, as if at the helm
fragrance soothing, soft petals caressing, thorny is the stem;

Frequented eagerly in throngs by all, age not the barrier
maidens pretty, demure, blushing, innocent like the flowers
some jogging, many walking, the lovers whispering, talking
a spectacle extraordinary, effort of so many, synergizing;

Spring it is, flowers full in bloom
celebrations and flower-shows, in boom
the park bedecked, participants straining
management in euphoria, compliments raining;

Huddled in a corner, the 'malis' sit in a bunch
crackling hands, sunken cheeks, bent, with a hunch
smiling with disdain, recall their stress and strain
in tending and nurturing the plants, in heat, chill or rain
alas! in the revelry, none notice their effort, or their pain.

***

57

Glory to Ye, O Moon

Glory to you, O moon! you hold sway
shining through, the night ever slipping away
glory for your lasting splendour
smilingly yielding, to the rising sun's grandeur;

Glory for you, for shining through the night
illuminating the horizon yonder, bright
splashing your silver, reflecting, refracting
soothing, cajoling, the lovers huddling;

Glory for your patience, to hide and bide
only to return, after the sun has retired
who knows, what quarter, will you be in
waxing or waning;

Will you return, with the same luster
controlled by the celestial cluster
even you know not
full or half and which half;

Who will see you and how will you be
appearing different, at different places
different, in different seasons
different even in time, what be the reason;

Glory to you O moon! for your patience
yet you never lose your cadence
even when masked, by low clouds tiny
yet giving us hope, by your silver lining;

The birds long to fly to you
the waves yearn to reach you
you embody love and romance
though distant, yet close to our hearts;

You are the beacon, for lovers
inspiring love, triggering the shivers
lovers longing, yearning for their love
naïve are you, know not, who makes you blush.

***

58

I Attended My Friend's Funeral

He chose to cut short his sojourn
his stopover in thy world, only to learn
he chose his time, to join ye, from this din
timely for him,but not so, for his kin;

He was finally content and at peace
a lasting smile, he adorned at ease
smilingly he left, smiling with disdain
on futility of it all, the pleasures and pain;

May be, he stood observing his own funeral
observing the agony, he caused for one and all
may be, he relented or resented his choice, if at all
to leave, stride away from the rest, firm in resolve;

Did he know, this was, a one way journey
did he know, he could not, reverse this itinerary
I wonder, was it his choice by design
or ye allured him, by thy aura divine;

They say, there is a long tunnel to cross
the heavenly abode, is a long way to pass
the pain disappears, as one transcends the threshold
the mystery remains, as none has returned to unfold;

Lord, thy ways do enthrall
thou prophesize, to protect us all
yet, ye allow the misery and pain to stretch
to extend unabated on the very people, thou protect;

My friend was healthy, wealthy and wise
he did leave a mark and not leave otherwise
I wonder whom he would have loved to carry along
all those to him, or all those to whom, he did belong;

Softly, a strange thought crossed my mind
if I was to be in his place, what would I find
am I a somebody, would I too be remembered indeed
hollow I feel, I am nobody yet, I better quickly rise in my deed.

***

59

And Then It All Looked So Clear

I chanced upon a visit, with my kin
to the shrine, of the nuclear medicine
to burn out, with precision so precise
spiteful cells, multiplying as if in a hive;

Muffled silence, packed with anxiety and hope
if sucked in by the disease, was there any scope
anxiety, if yet to decide, would it, or would it not be
many in ignorant bliss, as if it would never be;

The feelings were mixed, some content some resigned
some confident, some withdrawn, some distraught in mind
some in pain, some yet to be in, some recovering, resurrecting
some quiet, visibly affected, families supportive, interacting;

Strange I thought, disease so rampant, yet no solution in sight
research so much, laurels for many, yet none getting it right
stem cell therapy and genetic modification, may have a way
how and when, till then, many continue to suffer, all the way;

The sufferance is universal, for all efforts in vain
enhanced by the process itself, to remove the very pain
I happened to visit, yet higher such a shrine, a simple query
a revelation! none was cured, prolonged and palliative it be;

If above was to be true then why be in worry
go one has to, live every moment, as if in a hurry
a battle to fight within, but with a strategy,
battle of psychology and not, as of a tragedy;

Many have undergone, such a pain
yet lived a full life, lived not just in vain
those who give up, succumb without a fight
why not follow the heart, if guarantee is not in sight;

And then it looked so clear, a thought in mind
what would it be, if the turn was to be mine
given a choice, I would, if detected the last
to give not much time, for anxiety to last
reluctant I would be, to take the beaten path
enjoy the moments one can and merrily depart.

***

60

Hey Summer, Do You Remember

Hey Summer do you remember, when you came
jumping out of the basket, agile was your frame
taking a round, surveying, sniffing, absorbing
feeling at home and finally, condescending;

Graceful, yet naughty, elegant, but no let up
straight from the heaven, you hardly were a pup
you licked every one, as you sauntered in, on all fours
as our very own, soon you were christened, Summer;

With time you learned the tricks, to tease, as if feigning
your naughty pranks and wonderful skills in training
discipline, obedience, search, all these, in your stride
lab, for the lady of the house, but ye turned otherwise;

You displayed, canny and uncanny abilities, so rare
of intelligence, love, warmth, disarming was your stare
no wonder, all doted on you, yet you had us all, on our toes
beautiful eyes, grace, poise, as if on the ramp, would you pose;

With time, imperceptible was the change, in your heart
me in focus, possessive you became and took charge
curling up, compulsive in my presence, anxious, when not
my stress buster ye became, mental relief, you brought;

In time you had a family of your own, each one your look alike
to see our pup in its chores so motherly, what a pretty sight
who taught you all this, our Master, it is all your wonder
this wonderful creation, spellbinding in its splendour;

Reveling in your charms, we thought, it would last life long
life long it would, but canine life indeed, is not so long
with time you aged faster than us, the humans, I did realise
under the knife, in pain, I wondered, how the time had gone by;

You did pull through fine and were back in style
more humane than us, ever making us smile
the least you deserve, is a life much longer yet
you are no longer a pet, I wonder who is whose pet.

***

61

But For Thee

But for thee, I would have been, but me
but for thee, my life would have been mine
I love to live, every moment in spree
but all the moments that I live
are but borrowed from thee;

Is it thee, who keeps me going
is it for thee, my thoughts are flowing
is thy memory, engulfing my mind
or our moments together, to remind;

Is it love or passion, I know not
is it devotion to thee, I know not
but why does my heart miss a beat
if thy thought flashes, even in my sleep;

Be it love or not, but a wonderful feeling it is
a feeling so serene, nurtured deep within
a feeling of surrender, a feeling divine
keeps me entranced and ever on a high;

I was living, even before thee
an eventful life, my mind was free
new meaning to life, thou gave me
now all my roads, head towards thee;

Be in subconscious, thou were a part of me, for ever
deep down in my heart, waiting only, for a trigger
and then thou stepped out, ushering thy aura and charm
thy image in my thought, though deprived I am, of thy form;

Though away from thee, I have risen to rise
in my struggle, in my success and otherwise
my memory fades, thy thoughts ever with me
yet I continue to live in hope to be with thee;

Who controls my life, O! my love divine
beyond my control, is this love of mine
like a breath of fresh air, it is for me
I wonder, what would I be, but for thee.

***

62

The Prayer

They pray often
they pay their obeisance
they sing the hymns, they chant the mantras
they worship the Lord, alone or together in their own way;

They are devotional, they beseech, they sway
they fancy thee O Lord, in thy honour, they say
they appeal, they supplicate, they seek thy bliss
the rituals, the ceremonies, so elaborate to miss;

They are learned, they know the scriptures
they are the custodians, they control the access
they lay the rules, of how to, when to and where to pray
I watch them from a distance, I don't know what to say;

I am shy, I am mute, I am alone, I am ignorant
I know nothing, how to seek, to appease, I am reluctant
I peep within, a simple query, why so selfish I must be
why am I ever seeking, something or the other from thee;

I often reflect, do I have faith to seek thee the truth that be
do I believe in thy concept, power, image or blindly in thee
I know not where to seek thee, the shrines, litany or the liturgy
in the expanse of thy creation, I wonder where thou might be;

Are thou an image, an idol, a book or mystical power afar
or a fanciful creation, of our own euphemistic thought
no wonder, there are many, who question thy being to be
atheists some, but agnostics many, seeking rationale of thee;

Thy image is ever elusive, I give up my search for thee
why am I so shy to sing, the hymns, the mantras, in prayer to be
why I am so shy, in the rituals, as others, as if they know thee
in a corner, I close my eyes, to feel, what otherwise I cannot see;

And then, a mystical surge, flashes across my heart
thou are omnipresent, to seek thee, I don't have to go far
thou are omniscient, in prayers, I don't have to say it all
thou are omnipotent, in asking thee, I don't have to feel small
shy no longer, I now pray, simple, but straight from the heart.

***

63

A Mountain Stream

Rhythmic splash, of the curling stream
naughty wind, teasing, fondly caressing
folklore of pretty maidens, audible afar
ambience out of this world, as if in a dream;

I sit by its side upstream, watching the flow
my gaze following, slipping, as far as it can go
why this hurry, to leave me, or for someone ahead
I lose myself, in ecstasy of its splendour, instead;

Am I getting attached, to this fleeting flow
knowing that, I can hardly, even make it slow
how can I stem it, as its very life, is its flow
why I yearn for, what cannot be mine, be it so;

The stream is naïve, it knows not, where it is heading
to be engulfed by a rivulet or to its end, so dreading
to surrender to its destiny and lose its very being
to merge or be trapped and no more to be seen;

Sometime I fancy, the stream is in love
in love with whom, lavishing her curves
with the rivulet ahead, or the river thence
yet all flows, lead to the oceanic expanse;

Whatever be its end, the stream is full of life
bubbling, splashing, transparent, nothing to hide
short lived be the journey, yet cares not much it so
continues to lavish her freshness, brightening the show;

Sometime I wish, I too were a stream
meandering fearlessly, proudly would I beam
showering my charms on one and all, I would gleam
short may be the life, but worthwhile would it seem;

Pure and selfless, are the streams to mention
let all such streams flow, without inhibition
let none pollute them and stem their mission
let them thrive and be reflective of thy creation.

***

64

Were You to Return

Burying the past, I did muster, to get on afresh
overcoming your memory, new vistas shining ahead
life became beautiful once again, as if all was well
every day was new, full of hope, the time was swell;

All this lasted, for a long time and more
until, you resurfaced, shaken was I, to the core
my mind went in a tail spin, heart already taking control
life flashing back, I had missed you, with heart and my soul;

All this, so sudden, things were happening too fast
a longing long lost, too close, yet you were my past
the moments together, no more, life had rendered us apart
heart wanting, mind withholding, in dilemma was my thought;

I recall, the pleasure and pain, of love and separation
your presence or absence, was the source of my inspiration,
love kept me going, became my reason to survive
I allow it to float, you or your image, the time may decide.

***

65

And Then We Drifted Away

Do you remember,
our small world
binding us together,
the wind flowing
softly caressing;

Do you remember,
rhythmic it was
chiming of the chime,
the musical note afar
sending shiver up the spine;

Do you remember,
the crimson splash
of the receding sun,
in warmth of your love
new life, just begun;

Do you remember,
the moonlit night
in its silvery shine,
nothing we spoke,
just the sensation,
said it all, in no time;

Time, surely passing fast
until the moment came,
but life thereafter
was never the same;

Was it your compulsion,
or I went my way,
unable to fathom,
my memory fails
and then we drifted away.

***

66

I Am Ever In Competition

I am ever in competition
ever since I recall
competing in my first rise
and even in my first fall;

Competing, to speak monosyllables early
competing, to speak bi-syllables early
competing, to make sentences early
competing, to even chatter early;

I am ever in competition
to learn ahead, of my peers
to be a step forward, for sure
be it in any field, with or without tears;

My school bag, is in utter confusion
I am running, from tuition to tuition
winding, unwinding, learning, unlearning
conflicting thoughts, keep my mind churning;

I do have, my share of successes
but in plenty too, are the reverses
thrill I don't feel, I am as if in a groove
I am being pushed for ever, to further improve;

I am, their prized possession
to be boasted about, to be talked about
I have to outperform, my own potential
I ever have to rise, beyond their expectation;

I am, thus ever in competition
I have to run and continue to run
faster and faster, why! I am at a loss
against me myself, who all and what for;

Sometimes I feel tired and weary
tired of pushing the graphs, so dreary
ever on the edge, I have results, ever to give
whither the charm of life, I think, I forgot to live.

***

67

I Waited for Thee

I waited for thee, at the appointed hour
I waited for thee, at our favourite corner
the wait stretching, the eyes wandering
no sign of thee, the wait was unending;

Mind weary, yet hope was simmering
the next puff of breeze, may usher thee in
hoping, the next foot fall, may be thine
alas! in vain, was I to lose thee, with time;

Many a thought did cross my mind
how life without thee, would I find
painful is the pain of thy separation
thou are for ever, in my imagination;

I recall, our heavenly moments shared
thy fragrance and grace, filling the air
thy touch triggering the shivers, instead
not a word, yet so much would be said;

Is it with pain or pleasure, that I relive our moments
pleasure though short lived, yet lingering in my thoughts
pain though painful, yet welcome, as it reminds me to be
which one dominates, the pleasure or pain, both lead to thee;

Immersed in thy thoughts, I decide
to continue, yet excel, in my deeds beside
to struggle, to strive, and push myself, to rise
not to languish in thy memory, but to keep it alive;

Is it love, devotion, for my love or the divine
is it physical, platonic or spiritual, all blend so fine
whatever feeling it may be, but it holds me in awe
pure at heart and selfless is the surrender, to my love;

With all my love, I continue to wait
the feeling of love, is the feeling divine
I pray for strength, to continue to be
and be worthy of my love, if not to thee.

***

Section – III

Light for My Soul

68

Light for My Soul

Lights and lights, I see around
am bedazzled by the flash and sound
people, reveling and rejoicing in festivity
but my soul remains, bereft of any luminosity;

Alone in the reverberations, that surround
lost am I, in the noise and the din around
observing, relating, digesting, debating
my soul, masked by the veil, so descending;

Sparkling lights, near and far
darkness persisting, the doors ajar
all seem thrilled, the spirits so high
my soul suffers unlit, I know not why;

Celebrations here, festivity in the air
spirits on a high, feeling of joy so rare
the hearts in unison, with the souls
but my soul, languishes as before;

Untouched, by the external lighting
darkness within, is so frightening
kindle the flame of life, I pray
resurrect me, let light fall my way;

Allow me, to view and scroll
through the chasms of my soul
the truth, the pleasure and the pain
to revel in love and live not just in vain;

Let my soul retain, the purity as afore
let my soul be free to fly and soar
not in the hollowness, of the festivity
but in love, compassion and sensitivity;

Let thy light penetrate, my soul
let thy aura, engulf me in your fold
let me lose myself, to just be about
for those sans light, within or without.

***

69

The Look That I Cannot Forget

Lasting has been the imprint
of many a look, as I think
but your departure, I recall with regret
your parting look, I can never forget;

Depth of that look was mesmerizing
answering some, but more questions arising
was it love, but you looked away in haste
what was your quest, I am unable to state;

You chose to go, the call was thine
I was a mere bystander, a victim of time
your look, expressive, repenting, relenting
moments spent in love, was it relating;

I close my eyes and think of the past
that look, keeps flashing back in my heart
what was that, your look was putting across
was it me alone, or us, co-sufferers of this loss;

Why could life not take a new turn
why could you, in my life not return
why this pain, why within, must I burn
I wonder, how was my look, back in return;

Watching, the rhythmic fall of the rain
droplets, dripping down the window pane
I live in my world in vain, in hope I rest
neither you, nor that look, am I able to forget.

***

70

Time

Time and tide wait for none
success only, when its time has come
it is what I seek, am ever falling short of time
long is the journey of life, steep is the climb;

Clock keeps ticking, ever slipping is time
ere one knows, one is sliding past his prime
time spent in pain, lingers all the time
time in love, though short, lasts a life time;

Stretching my imagination, to move against the flow
to tread the path untrodden, though movement be slow
my mind, yearns to soar like a bird, in this journey of life
pitch my aims high, succeed or not, time only will decide;

Sometimes I ask, what exactly is, that we call, time
is it absolute, relative, referral or a measure of the chime
is it by the sun, the day, the hours or the moments, so to say
hour glass, clocks, pendulum, crystal, now atomic, all in fray;

Some believe, time is cyclical, as be the wheel of time
some believe, time is linear, there will be, the end of time
some believe, there is appointed time, for every event in life
vice like grip, unnerving is the stranglehold, exerted by time;

Sometimes I reflect, it is time, to be rid of clutches of time
be indifferent, is the first thought, that comes to my mind
let my thoughts be afloat, my deeds to follow the same line
just do my bit and ignore the rest, let the pace set be mine;

Sounds simple, but is working, at peace are my heart and soul
time to catch up with my inner self, to dream and yet more
I slip into a reverie, simmers still, the flame of love in my heart
dormant for long, now resurfaces, time was tearing me apart;

Now all is tranquil, time, has come to a stand still
fired by love, I have now, the raison d' etre to live
I am now at ease, transported as if, back in time
a simple thought, has changed this life of mine.

***

71

If All Goes Well

If all goes well, life would be fun
pace would be mine, no need to run
I would rise, beyond what I had sought
life too may respond, as I had thought;

Vibrant in youth, lofty in my dreams
aspirations surging, bursting at the seams
arduous was the path, yet spirits were alive
if all goes well, I thought, limit be the sky;

Was I naïve, or innocent in my thought
was I foolish, or seeking beyond my spot
was I assuming, or living in my dream
honest in effort, to seek glory and esteem;

The reality dawned, as the time was passing
some was, but a lot more not my way, in the offing
was I ambitious, or my sights pitched too high
did I waver, or lose my focus, I can but give it a go by;

Now that present is past, I sit back and reflect
life has given me a fair deal, may not the best
what if, I was granted a boon, to seek my quest
I could hardly define, the ideal in my interest;

Would I seek health, wealth or to be wise
would I seek my love, to be ever by my side
contentment or happiness, lasting, to what end
the list would be long, but the answers, distant;

As I think along, the mystery unfolds
what one gets, is relative, one may conjure
one may excel, yet, some one will still be ahead
would it be cause for thrill, or unhappiness instead;

The years have gone by, I peep down my past
all must have gone well, so much have I got
endless could be the need, but should it be so
what I did not get, I did not miss, to be my motto.

***

72

A Rogue Heart

Tucked somewhere in my ribcage
size of my fist, snug in the lungs, they say
chambers four, with valves controlling the flow
one half to receive, the other, for pure blood to go;

Keeps beating all the time
in low times and times prime
for whom it beats, it asks me not
my control hardly any, though it is my heart;

Triggered it is, by some electrostatic shots
its beat better be normal, if I were to last
it decides its pace, sensing my stress
how to control it, I know less and less;

Wandering, in collusion with my eyes
lurks on any pretty thing, under the sky
surprise in store, when I take a stock
only to find, that I have lost my heart;

To whom did I lose and why, I draw a blank
blindly it drives me, no option, thanks to my heart
love, compassion, consideration for many, emotions rare
feelings it evokes, even if these lead to pain, it hardly cares;

Sometimes I think, it is time I was in control
I have a life of my own, many a thought to dispose
my memories, my reminiscences, my love and my past
wither to store, there is no spare chamber in my heart;

As I reflect, a fresh thought comes to my mind
why not be natural, allow my heart to be of its kind
let my memories and thoughts, be one with my heart
it has kept me going, even if a rogue has been my heart;

Life now is at peace, way behind is the conflict
I see what my heart sees, I feel what my heart feels
mellowed by this thought, I feel I am now better off
I hold back nothing, now I speak straight from the heart.

***

73

Those Eyes

Powerful are those eyes
ever holding me in sway
transfixed I remain
unable, to take my gaze away;

Those eyes, are not there for merely to see
reflect they thy thoughts and mind, so I feel
expressive they are, beyond imagination
so much they convey, by mere expression;

Are they black, brown or hazel
unable to conjure, I am bedazzled
once thou cast thy gaze upon me
entranced, I slide into a reverie;

Sometimes, I try to probe thy look
is it a mere scan, or open like a book
is it thy love, your eyes wish to convey
as I look back, teasingly they shy away;

Often I feel, even when in a crowd
thy eyes seeking mine, I feel proud
once in sight, fondly caressing as never before
thrilled within, I can feel their warmth and more;

Do thy eyes express thy love, I know not
do they hide behind thy love, I can guess not
I get a feeling, they seek me to be with thee
why the shiver up my spine, if love it not be;

Are thy eyes under thy control, I wonder
are they on their own, for this visual plunder
do they move with or without any concern
eagerly my eyes too, seek them in return;

Haunted in my dreams, I am by thy eyes
power of thy look, I still love to live by
thy eyes, playing hide and seek, all the time
if love it is, then let it be, be my love divine.

***

74

Have My Thoughts Dried

Have my thoughts dried, have I said it all
I am but a pale shadow of mine, who stood so tall
is it a passing phase, or a matter for keeps
wither my freshness, I search, I trace no beeps;

Bundles of energy, adrenaline flowing, mind ever on fire
thoughts flourishing, a-brim was the cup, to my heart's desire
freshness in thought, ideas in the mind sprouting beside
love, romance, nature, myriad topics, all would strike;

What happened, to the spring of my thoughts
unending was the flow, why am I now distraught
life so smooth, all at peace, wither have all these gone
shaken I am, writhing in pain as if lost in love, or lovelorn;

Was the fire fuelled within, by my love for thee
intense was the intensity, a source of inspiration, for me
was the separation from thee, my raison d' etre to be
nothing has changed, I am groping, why all this to me?

With glisten in the eye, I would be alive to the matters of life
deep, intent, close to my heart, would be the struggle and strife
compassion would engulf my thought, for those in deprivation
why have I retracted to my shell, why this exasperation?

Retrograde is this state, how have I fallen in total disarray
I must unwind, rewind and do whatever to undo, I can but pray
freshness must return, emotions too, life is no life otherwise
fired by the resolve I introspect, what and why, how to revive;

I close my eyes, I reflect, how to go by
how to refresh and rekindle, the flame in my life
how to demystify the layers of mist, settled on my mind
I see a flash, the fog starts lifting, unfettering me from the bind;

What emerges is revealing, simple to state
I can't be running all the time, must slow down the pace
thoughts are slaves to none, they are like free birds, which soar
creativity is not against time, this is what comes to the fore
if these come natural to mind, epitome will be within reach
not easy to cultivate, excellence in thoughts none can teach
I decide to wait, for my thoughts to resurface from their retreat.

***

75

The Moorings

To face the world, one left early from the nest
to acquire and achieve, whatever be the best
bursting with energy, bubbling with dreams
to learn, to flourish, charmed by life, it seemed;

Maturing fast, bravely one faced life
a bold step, though too early, taken in a stride
did I lose childhood too soon, I knew not
stepping early into adulthood, a boon, I can say not;

The clock kept ticking and time kept slipping
much had been done, but much more to do
aspirations ever rising, the competition, not far behind
past though fading, but simmering deep in the mind;

Time flies, but love for my moorings, lingers
to the place, people or the ambience, I wonder
the people, have changed, new faces make me a stranger
the place looks different, familiarity to ambience in danger;

Why do I crave to be in the past, strange, I think
I wasn't the best nor the brightest, so why this blink
was it the warmth of the folks, the kin or friends galore
was it the love initiated, fascinating dreams and nothing more;

I close my eyes and think, were the moments worthy, or in vain
the moments past, relating to the streets, the lanes, the by-lanes
the hills, trees, the meadows, some real, some deep in my mind
my memories buried within, with nostalgia, I try to unwind;

I look inwards and continue to probe, what was so different
the sky was different, the moon so close, the sun so elegant
the winds caressing, the stars familiar, as if shining for me alone
tender moments of love, a world though small, but my very own;

All is not a mere dream, nor was it just ethereal
the bonding pure, one pines for the life so real
this may be my way to unwind, I feel like a child
recharged, my moorings transport me, back in time.

***

76

My Fading Memory

Bags of memories, memorable some, least to say
cherish my early years, plenty attention, my way
exciting was life, romance too in the air
love not far behind, moments so rare;

Yet many more in store, that I love to retrace
buried deep in my heart, eagerly waiting to surface,
trigger for these be thee, happy moments that we spent
in a world of our own, we were a perfect blend;

I fondly recall, refreshing walks in the rain
so enervating, instant relief, from any strain
and then you drifted away, also did recede thy image
reducing to a mere dot, why so, my memory fades;

Life though different, but continued in thy absence
thy memory apart, started afresh, as if with vengeance
harnessing my energy, whizzing past like a blaze
did thy love inspire me, or not, here my memory fades;

Life has given me all, much more may come by
flourished in heart and soul, inspired, to do or die
fresh challenges every day, urge to excel in this race
thy absence, a boon! can hardly conjure, my memory fades;

My fading memory, apparently a great help
a facilitator it is, as many a moment, I rather forget
for better or worse, I know not what may be true
to forget misery of my past, it comes to my rescue;

Sometimes I wonder, if I could control my memory
selective I rather be, release the chambers, at will
recall the moments one loved, revel in that state
erase the rest from my heart, or let my memory fade.

***

77

The Autumn

Variety is the spice of life, so they say
so bring the seasons, annually our way
cyclical they are, with regularity they come
ushering in pleasure and joy, at least for some;

Simple is the effect, yet so complex the cause
the planet rotating, revolving on the elliptical path
on a tilt, that too varying, we traverse the solar orbit
uneven exposure, the differential triggers, the seasonal shift;

Temperate if we remain, the seasons are four, to stay
the summer, generous in the energy, that it permeates
the farmers love it, the seeds that it so germinates
melting snow gushing down, we love and adulate;

The winter, though cold, but many love it, still
cosying up, love and romance, beats the chill
the spring, the darling of all, a poet's delight
flowers a-bloom, merrily everything comes alive;

Following the summer, the autumn is on the scene
trudging, trailing, drooping with guilt, it may seem
paving the way for harsh chill, warmth fast in retreat
trees denuded, ambience melancholy, barren are the streets;

Poor autumn, not so popular with many
twilight it portrays, of this seasonal cacophony
rustle of the leaves, carpeting the paths
crackling is the sound, some like it not;

Myriad thoughts flash across my mind
viewed differently, unique is autumn to find
what a maze of colours, some trees adorn
festive, for Thanks Giving and Halloween to crown;

I sit back and reflect, on this autumnal thought
twilight of the cycle it is, I too am in a similar spot
in autumn of life, I too am braving to take it in my stride
as new cycle for the seasons, to new life, I too will eagerly slide.

***

78

Land of Our Rising Sun

Yes thou are, the land of our rising sun
way to the east, mystic Arunachal, but none
our first tip, lit by the golden splash of the dawn
rightly named are thee after the sun, lavish in crimson

Fascinating amalgam of nature, are thee
lush green forests, deep and dense, an explorer's spree
deep down thy valleys, filled with vibrant rivers, from the peaks
pure and emerald is the aqua, the rivulets, rhythmic in speech;

Vast expanse of lush, one but breaks into a song
rare are the myriad orchids and the rhododendrons
colorful flowers, dotting the stretches verdant
a unique mix of the hues, on display to glance;

Meandering paths, overlooking are the tall pines
a sight out of the world to view, in posture supine
the silvery clouds mystic, as if floating below
inviting to step out, and feel the rainbow;

Thin is the populace, but wonderful they are
tribes are many, unique in language and attire
pure and innocent, warm and affectionate, they are
reaching out by habit, yet their solitude, they so desire;

Content are thy people, religious in mind
co-exist all in harmony, with no axe to grind
some follow the Buddha, some pray to nature
some follow their elders, differences none, so mature;

Inaccessible are thy interiors, massive efforts are on
so much done, much more yet, in feverish hurry are some
bubbling are the youth, yearning to reach the sky
education, as if has taken wings, they wish and aim high;

Come festivities, unbridled is the deluge, of colour and dance
petite belles, demure, martial arts on display, rare sight to glance
seeing them so engrossed, a thought does cross my mind
flourish they should, yet retain their heritage, so rare to find.

***

79

The Soldier

Upholds, sanctity of our borders
if called upon, maintains law and order
upholds, integrity of our constitution
proud am I, to be a soldier of this elite institution;

Fire in the belly, bubbling with energy
I worked hard, to be found worthy
young was I, aspirations riding high
rigorous the training, aimed for the sky;

A soldier am I, wiry and athletic, a young man
proud of my medals and the accoutrement
chest filled with pride, head held high
honour of my country, I protect all the time;

Unmindful, of my personal comfort
warmth, of my home and hearth
I serve with élan, to keep the flag high
hesitate will I not, for the supreme sacrifice;

I forgo my freedom,
of thought, speech and action
disciplined to lead and be led to fight
never to question the reason, but do and die;

I face the challenges, with a smile
vagaries of weather, enemy, in a stride
I go, where I am asked to go
areas far-flung, bounded by snow;

In solitude, I remain
in surveillance, of my domain
loneliness, does come my way
hail, rain or sunshine, I must keep awake;

I am ever a-smile, never feel depressed
privations I ignore, posing problems, I resist
I ignore, if furtherance, does not come my way
when time, I quietly walk out and fade away;

Now that the time has gone by
so much water has flown in life
I sit back and reflect, to take a stock
in life, what I gained and what I lost;

I recall, working conditions, so harsh
minor error, even in line of fire, the law took charge
in defending others, I hardly thought of my own defence
the castration so harsh, even for a minor offence;

Fortunate I feel, to be alive and in one piece
harsh was the journey, the path too steep
all that glittered once, no longer on the scene
left to fend for myself, life seems grim;

I now find basic issues, staring me in the face
food, shelter, schooling, health, difficult to chase
when I was risking my life, others in comfort
deployed afar, someone kept me out of the loop;

I missed, seeking my share of the pie
at the mercy of those, who never took a risk in life
and those I defended, were casting the dice
now that I am out, I am on my own
a soldier no more, but a veteran;

But I ignore, I continue to live with dignity
intact are the values, the truth not yet lost to me
I am a fast learner, I stretch my self, only to what I need
richness is embedded, in my thoughts and in my deed.

***

80

After You Left Me

After you left me, abruptly midstream
I remained in shock, a tragic tale, did it seem
did you think of me, when you chose to go
and about our wards, who had yet to grow;

Happy were all, in your return from afar
loaded with gifts, for one and all,
in gratitude, in a hurry, you left for the shrine
never to return, in one stroke, shattering this world of mine;

When I was rejoicing in delight, eagerly waiting for thee
did I know, you lay writhing in pain, your return, never to be
inconsolable was I, overtaken by the events, but little could I do
the journey of life staring, how would I traverse, I had no clue;

The days of luxury over, the struggle, now begun
gather my wits, to face the world, I was the one
to pick up threads, from where you had left
uninitiated was I, had to learn it all afresh;

They say, time is a great healer
in my case, it was, but a mere squealer
pain persisting, within and without
I was patient, hoping some solace to sprout;

Sometimes I think, why so much pain and misery my way
what wrong had I done, why this penalty, I had to pay
I thought our union made in heaven, was noble and pure indeed
the stars all matched and vibrant, so were we, in word and deed;

Hardened am I, in thought, as the time has flown
I too have learnt to smile, at least on my own
I have not lost hope, surely, the times will turn
I too will get a reprieve, happy will be this sojourn;

I think of you with love, I reflect but never repent
happy moments we shared, though short, but none to relent,
strengthened by your love and so true an advice
there are many more in misery, I step out, only to realise;

I have done what I could, life has gone by
I am grateful, for the grit and the will to strive
life could have been better, but it has given me a go by
yet ungrateful am I not, committed to the needy, the deprived.

***

81

The House Wife

I would often dream, when I was young
to dream like a princess, a flower in the spring
my prince charming, waiting somewhere
to woo me, win me and earn my love to share;

Bubbling with energy and vigour, I lived my life
pretty girl was I, graceful in poise, natural in stride
thrilled by nature, the flowers and their bloom
every day new, tender was my heart, free from gloom;

I grew to be a young lady, my dreams, still there
a prince charming my folks did find, was he, rare
I still loved my life, was innocent in my thought
wonderful it was, to care, to seek and be sought;

A family we became, I matured fast
assuming a fresh role, unwinding from my past
transiting from a free bird, to run the house and care
showering my all on my nest, with no time to spare;

I learned to understand, the struggles of life
of my wards, our folks and my role as a wife
stress and strain of all, would fall in my lap
humble effort to relieve them, bridging the gap;

Rarely did I think, of myself and my need
happy and content, to see them succeed
time flew, my energy dwindled, with time
lo behold, I was sliding past my prime;

Startled was I, it was time, to reflect
how the life has gone by, am unable to react
housewife, house maker or a mere housekeeper
all busy with their lives, do I sense a feeling of neglect;

What happened to my dreams, what have I done all along
have I squandered my years, and given my life for a song
the mystery unfolds, there is yet another way, to look at it all
one has created life, taken care, in their eyes, I still stand tall;

Deep in satisfaction, I break into a smile
a task well done and accomplished well in time
free to live my life, plenty done, plenty yet to name
in the calculation of life, loss far outweighed by the gain.

***

82

The Eclipse

Lost in my thoughts, I look at the sky
wither the sun, the moon has given it a go by
hemmed in between, new moon has cast its shadow
mighty sun eclipsed, yet amber within, retains its glow;

Surprised, by the celestial interplay
restive is the sun, amused, at its fate
its splendour and grandeur, under a veil
transitory though, yet its brightness curtailed;

The environs illusive, night as if, has descended
birds in disarray, their day's quest, as if ended
confused they are, by this nocturnal effect
head back to their nests, their needs, hardly met;

The shadow, is in transit
long, does not it last
but leaves an effect, lasting
the mighty too, can be overcast;

This sets me thinking
I look within, I think of my thoughts
can I hold myself, influence if be brought
or do I succumb, to an overbearing thought;

I smile as I go deeper, in the journey of my past
infallible is none, there is ever yet, a bigger star
only if, one can decide and follow, not the trodden path
like sun, eclipsed be only in visage, let none eclipse thy heart.

***

83

Empowered By Loss of Power

A long innings, time to call it a day
friends many, soon, we had to part our ways
a bubbling adolescent, sucked up by the tunnel
fortunate to be unscathed, at the end of the tunnel;

Overwhelmed was I, by the pleasure and the pain
the system fair, so were the colleagues in the chain
privilege to be in it, it had become a way of my life
inspired by the honest work, the head ever held high;

Rise I did up the ladder, was natural, no airs to name
feet firm, mind in balance, humble, I still remained
then came the proverbial day, to leave all this behind
emptiness staring, many a thought, flashed in mind;

Mentally prepared, yet shaky, the morning after
from somebody to nobody, a turn in life, thereafter
the preparations, deliberations, not coming forth
traumatic, yet one had to be, the same as before;

With time, confidence restored, in new life to be
heralding the new found freedom, wonderful to feel
time flying, mind soaring, creativity, close behind
packed routine, activities many, yet more in mind;

Empowered again, fresh energy, for my thought
plenty of books, sports, writing, life as I had sought
the needs not so great, finances thus in place
eager for life ahead, in intellect was my solace;

Moments many, but not a moment to spare
life, what a treat, so beautiful and so rare
power I lost, but that, never was mine, for sure
real power, lay in this empowerment of my soul.

***

84

And When You Came

Rolly polly were you, when you came
feast to our eyes, our new baby, to name,
always giggling, ever a-smile, even when in sleep
contented you appeared, a rare child to speak;

Rosy cheeks, chinky eyes, as if from the east
a beauty you were, chubby, very fond of sleep
kept us enthralled, your demure looks and pretty eyes
a baby with a difference, undemanding, rarely did ye cry;

Strange your ways, hissy noise, could hardly keep you awake
doting was your family, brother in toddle, parents in the wake
our life transformed, complete we became, excitement in the air
as you grew, your antiques kept us busy, with no time to spare;

Time flew by, ere we realized, you were in your teens
pretty maid you became, graceful, dignified and so keen
values of life you imbibed, we were unable to conjure
is it our little baby, so accomplished and so mature;

Natural in your ways, an elegant lady you became
prince charming came your way, love was in the air
lo behold! soon you were wed and gone from our nest
new vistas in your life, to your new family and the rest;

As the time goes by, amazing it is to see you flourish
the values yet stronger, natural and forthright, with finesse
meticulous effort to bring up your wards, worthy of acclaim,
I reflect, in my turn was not even close, leave alone the same;

We stand in awe and gratitude to Thee, our master
how you transformed a tiny baby, to a lady of charm
to a mother and to so many perfect a role, to name
innocent and pure as a child, at heart she still is the same;

She is unique to us, but is a revelation of thine
there are many more, who spread thy love divine
so much to learn from, so much to share
Lord give us her wisdom, compassion and the care.

***

85

O Ye Winter

O ye winter! you come with such regularity
cyclical are your visitations, entrenched in posterity
of late you have started shrinking, is it the global warming
getting used to, with less of you, makes you more charming;

What a change, with you around, woolens puffy and fluffy
coats, overcoats, caps, gloves, in many a layer, one is stuffy
maidens dressed in bright, looking elegant, what a sight
children, not lagging behind, dressed as if, birds in flight;

I fondly recall, what a dreamy time it was, in the hills
you ushered in freshness, tranquil and serene, to the heart's fill
in a reverie, to sit by the fireside and watch its embers glow
the flame, turning yellow to bluish, rising in its flow;

At your peak, you do display, your might
by sudden appearance, of the sheet of white
the flakes, soft and fleeting, as if in a stride
trees sprinkled, drooping, as in a painting bright;

You invigorate the energies, a feeling of well being
chill there is, harder can one work, no sweltering
appetite rising, urge for rich food and fries
the system responding, enabling long strides;

That was one world, my world, I never saw what lay beyond
there existed yet another, where winter held not much charm
the deprived, for those in the open, for those with no woolens
those with no fire, fire within, but none without, limbs swollen;

Awakened from my slumber, I shudder, but now I observe
a child reeling in the open, shivering, with nothing to preserve
an old man freezing, waiting, for this extravaganza to subside
hoping, the night will somehow pass, and there will be sunrise;

As if in a hurry, to do whatever I can, yet will all this suffice
a drop in the ocean it is, so many, one can hardly surmise
regretting, every moment that I relished, I am but in shame,
we have failed, I urge you divine lest you too feel the same.

***

86
The Centipede

A unique manifestation, of the life indeed
elongated is my body, I am the centipede
segmented am I, with a pair of legs for each
wobbly in move, takes time, for last legs to reach;

Flattened is my head, with antennae to feel
pincer like claws, help me trap my meal
venom in my gland, released on my prey
predator am I, for survival I have to slay;

Endowed with many a sensory limb, am I
in my face, head and the pair of legs behind
partially does it help, as seldom have I the eyes
nocturnal therefore, from the hawks, I must hide;

I have no spine, I am an invertebrate
but spineless I am not, intrusion I can't tolerate
I go in a frenzy, when I see the female of mine
courtship dance triggers, a shiver up my spine;

Small in size, but I can go up to an arm length
life span not so large, may be half a decade, depends
I loose water from my skin, I love to be in habitat moist
under the leaves, subterranean are my hides, not easy to hoist;

Sometimes I think, what good am I
drab to look at, appear slimy and sly
but not so, I contribute a lot in my humble way
I thrive on worms, the birds on me, eco balance I maintain;

I watch around and stretch my imagination beyond
if I were to dress up, designer will have a tough time
if I were to wear the shoes, for ever will I take to find
if I were to dance, my legs will be hard to unwind;

I cannot sit back, but I do reflect most of the times
what form of life am I, neither half nor full in my prime
what did I do to earn this life, I ask thee, my master
what good can I do to get out of this cycle, faster
unable to think, I wonder, when will I have my answer?

***

87

But for Noah's Ark

Deep in love, I sauntered down the vale
in a world of my own, dreaming of a mythical tale
eager to share with my love, I wish she was by my side
my mind soaring, thoughts too, taking long strides;

Lost in my thought, I go back in time
to the genesis of this world, by the Lord divine
what a wonder He created, out of chaos, in no time
just Adam and Eve, immortalized, but with no life line;

Destined to die, thanks to the fraud serpentine
Satan persuasive, forbidden tasted, naïve Eve fell in line
Adam too plunged, sapient in thought, but deep was his love
love satiated, but guilt & regret, became their anguishing trove;

Thus commenced the beginning of the end
fall from the image, wickedness was the trend
divine wrath, fell on all, thus did the deluge start
perished all save those, aboard the Noah's Ark;

Life started afresh, world grew in haste
forbidden now nothing, joy of love, could one taste
man grew, from strength to strength, nothing left to relent
chasing success, generations over, intelligent was the descent;

I now reflect, time has gone by, we have come afar
modern has become life, facilities for one and all
love too has flourished, so much of give and take
norms for some, many a form now, for love to relate;

Strange be the thought, if Eve, had remained chaste
forbidden fruit untouched, if none were to taste
would there still be a deluge, would life restart
but ordained was it so, Adam and Eve had to go
gratified we be, none be here but for Noah's Ark.

***

88

The Wedding

Mammoth gathering, festivity in the air
wedding in being, full of glitter and glare
friends, kin jostling, for a glimpse of the pair
the newly weds lost, in the flash and stare;

Young couple, presenting a wonderful sight
bedecked, bejeweled, looked elegant and bright
the parents beaming, hovering, full of affections
hospitality flowing, the details tied to perfection;

The bride and groom, befitting the pedestal
sharing their dreams, for future, eager to fulfill
a-smile, full of charm, it is the event of their life
anxious to take the plunge, to be man and wife;

The bride, looking demure, calm and serene in poise
the thoughts of the future, the unknown, the life and joy
many a thought crossing her mind, yet unable to say
to leave her nest, kith and kin, to live the life, not her way;

The bride thinking, would her life be, unfettered and free
would she be loved still, if in love, if not, how would it be
would there be a place for love, or lost to love, would she be
would the new life be conducive, what if, if it was not to be;

All these thoughts, the bride had deliberated, at length before
but these were now going to be for real, just a step more
with the preparations, the celebrations and the guests galore
no turning back, alas! alternate thoughts, she had to ignore;

The groom too, had different thoughts, churning in his mind
how would his wife be, a friend, companion, would she be kind
would this, be the end of his freedom, his activities, no more
be sucked in the grind, be just the provider and nothing more;

All the thoughts about the wedlock, conflicting, yet so real
none can guarantee the future, yet marriage, is a good feel
ideal it can never be, it would always be, plenty of give and take
love may not be, but respect must be, true for all couples to be.

***

89

The Fish

Lost in my thoughts was I, by the river side
the emerald green water, sparkling, in the sun rise
what a scene to watch, the fish darting, far and near
a school of them, their purpose, only to them was clear;

Dreaming of my love, I would feed them, betimes
throngs of them would appear from nowhere, in no time
graceful in their move, dignified and elegant in their spree
awesome display, beauty of the nature, in its purity;

Spontaneous was it, a thought, flashed across my mind
how would it be, if I were a fish, to leave this life behind
swim uninhibited in the vast expanse, be a master of my time
simple life, free from stress and strain, of this world of mine;

Life different, under water, swimming all the time
breathe through the gills, steering with the fins, I won't mind
senses normal, olfactory, ocular and intelligence to state
minimal be the needs, would saunter at leisure, for my intake;

Fancy I would, if I were, a fish marine
to swim across the ocean, my heart would pine
if deep water I loved, I would dive to the abyss
stay nocturnal, the sunlight I would not miss;

If I were a shark, tuna or a swordfish
extremely fast would I be, not easy to be a dish
if gold fish I be, ornamental I would become
a fond pet I would be, the problems be none;

Sometimes I reflect, what a fish I would be
would I drink like a fish, or like myself would I be
troubled would be the waters, if fishermen, there be
would I be in comfort, or like a fish out of water would I feel;

I stretch my imagination, to say
how, if my love too, jumped in this fray
together we would swim, side by side
love would flourish, be it low or high tide
until a bigger fish or a net terminated this delight.

***

90

The Security Guard

In excitement of fresh avenues and allure of vistas unknown
to be someone, to earn with dignity and to be on my own
I ventured from my serene life, with a promise to be back
adrenaline flowing, bubbling, aspiring, to be on a fast track;

The big city I stumbled into, engulfed me, a culture of its own
life fast, ever on run, many people, strangers, unknown
relentless to pursue excellence, learn and practice hard
beaming with pride I announce, I am the new security guard;

Enamoured by the uniform spick and span
the peaked cap, the belt and the accouterment
the power and the authority to add, I had never seen before
in a world of dreams, I drifted until, the truth came to the fore;

I am a mere guard, one of many, in the campus to be
habitat though lush, but the inhabitants, indifferent to me,
I know them all, but seldom anyone notices me
I am like a fixture to them, to see through, but not to be seen;

I am fortunate, ever on duty, with little time to reflect
sometimes I do think, was this the life, to be lead
awake all night, sleepy all the day, yet sleep shying away
ever in disorientation, mixed up between night and day;

Yet there is much more to reflect, my life, a run of the mill
bereft of adequate knowledge and any professional skill
I live in deprivation, forced to share my bunk, with many
alternating day and night, all cutting costs, to the penny;

I live frugal, eat frugal, sleep frugal, all frugal, as if on a fast
save the most, sustain many back home, simple seems the cost
I yearn to see my folks, to revel in the serenity of life, that was
unable to pull out, I am their life line, even a day is their loss;

Alarmed, as I look into the mirror, the hard truth descends
I live like a robot, mechanical with no emotions to transcend
how long can I sustain, I look around, no hope, I am distraught
unable to find an alternative, but to be, a security guard.

***

91

Dreams That I Dream

I am a dreamer,
a dreamer of lofty dreams
I dream of a world, of camaraderie transcending
I dream of a world, of love and warmth descending;

I dream of a world, free from fear
I dream of a world, free from scare
I dream of a world, narrowing the gaps
between the haves and the have-nots;

I dream, where innocence of a child is not lost
where a child has it all in abundance and love is not short
where a child has toys to play, is adorned by a lingering smile
not where misery robs him of his childhood, by ruse and guile;

I dream of a world, where no one goes to sleep hungry
where no one is left in the open, to face nature's fury
where there is fair opportunity, to learn and share
where there is ample for all, yet sufficient to spare;

I dream for myself to rise, without treading on any toes
I dream to excel without usurping other's show
I dream to reach the lofty heights, by my own sweat and toil
I dream to grow, without infringing, anyone else's soil;

As time passes, strange thoughts cross my mind
are my dreams of this world, or of the world behind
are my dreams far fetched, utopian, foolish or more
if foolish it be to seek a smile for a child, let it be so;

At the crossroads I stand, perplexed
I muster all my inner strength, to flex
to follow my dreams or follow the beaten path
to shine the hard way, or stagnate, in luxury of the rot;

Oh Lord, give me the strength, to press on
to press on regardless, idolising the idealistic
following my dreams, I have still managed to stay
I rather get somewhere, if not in full, at least half the way.

***

92

Soothing Patter of the Rain

You are welcome, always and every time
you restore, our ever dwindling life line
you bring us joy, you bring us relief
soothing is your musical patter, even if brief;

The clouds precede your arrival
sometimes passing, sometime to stay
sometimes quiet, sometimes in thunder
imposing it is, the display of your splendour;

Laden winds arise, from the seas afar
when in transit, wispy vapourous you are
as you cool, you condense and precipitate to fall
water again, fulfilling the need, of one and all;

Sometimes you tiptoe, sometimes you are the power
sometimes you refresh, but sometimes you are on fire
sometimes you are soothing, but sometimes otherwise
sometimes you persist, lashing in fury, I wonder why;

You ever balance, the cycle of life, to adjust
your graceful presence, just about enough
unpredictable of late, has become your trend
too much, too late, or contrary, is the blend;

You control the life, of mortals
farmers look upwards, for their survival
alas! you have chosen to change your tack
topsy-turvy is their cycle, adverse is the impact;

I fondly recall mild drizzle of thine
patter on the window, tapping in rhyme
you fill the air with romance, for one and all
walking hand in hand, lovers lost in love, as you fall;

I love to be out, when you are around
splashing your charms, on those you abound
heavenly it is to see, your tiny drops at the tips
soothing is your patter, out of this world to miss.

***

93

Help Me My Master

With bowed head I seek
from thee, O Lord, I beseech
I am lost, where to search and see
help me, my Master, to find myself, for me;

Am I lost, in the wilderness
in the labyrinth, of worldly mess
in a temple, or in a shrine
seeking the truth, or thee divine;

Am I lost in my love, or seek the one, who may
am I hiding from myself, I find none, my way
am I lost in my thoughts, or in my deed
I know not, lost I remain, but indeed;

Pray, guide me, where to look for myself
in thy splendour in a valley, or in the misty hills afar
in the soft touch of my love, or in the wake of who may
or in the innocence of a child, whose smile makes my day;

Lost though, yet I remain in thy creation
I am there, yet not there, weird sensation
why this dilemma, sometimes I reflect
how to find myself and feel the impact;

I wonder, where should I be
in the arms of my beloved, may be
seeking knowledge or truth, could be
but lost I remain, wherever I be;

I fancy, I am a bird unfettered
I fancy, I could soar afar unhindered
to the lofty heights, I dreamt of beyond
alas! I remain fettered, to the worldly bonds;

I close my eyes and focus my thought
I find thee, my Master, my answer, I just got
easy it is to recall, your smile reveals it all
I have only to look inwards, I am not too far.

***

94

In Remembrance

You held my hand, all the way
ere from this life, you walked away
guiding me, beyond the horizon
on your footprints, I only wander;

I looked for you, hither and thither
to learn, I was to be on my own, I shiver
wondering, how would I face the world alone
bereft of your love and the touch, that I had known;

I recall your glimpse, I so admired
your reassuring aura, rekindled the fire
challenges I took, sans any fear and inhibition
face the world I did, with courage and conviction;

You taught me to balance, in my toddle and trot
to be content and be happy, with what one got
to strive but not to miss, if it was not to be
but miss I do, your glorious personality;

You ever watched me grow, with deep satisfaction
unobtrusive, stoic, open like a friend, in interaction
my every small step forward, was a joint leap for you
I couldn't have dared many such leaps, but for you;

I thought of you, as I grew
my prime, well behind me now
I ask myself, have I braced up to your scale
I feel your aura, in my success, or as I fail;

Time has flown, I have transited to the past
post the present, the future is stepping in fast
I am done, fading from the scene though
making way, for the next line to grow;

I reflect, would I be missed, like you
as your love, will my love, hold the sway too
would my footprints, also be worth treading on
will my deeds too inspire, answers I have none.

***

95

Is Love Blind

Is love blind, I often wonder
a feeling of ecstasy and surrender
is it for my love or thee, the mystery remains
feeling natural, the heart yields, unrestrained;

Love has no eyes, how does it see
why and how in love, there will never be
in love one questions not, love is supreme
one sees what one wants to, only love is the theme;

Love sure is blind, it holds the love high
to the flaws and follies, it turns a blind eye
love can do no wrong, its pedestal is sky high
it is a bonding of hearts, looks, are a mere go by;

As the summer wine, love matures with time
permeating down the heart, remains ever sublime
love is patience, love is endless wait, love is sacrifice
intense in love, the pleasure and pain, live side by side;

Love transcends the barriers, of caste and creed
love is compassion, a sensation, above all the needs
love sees its love everywhere, in everything, all the time
when in love, just close the eyes, one sees the love divine;

They say one falls in love, I wonder, is it so
feeling so pure and selfless, cannot be low
one has to rise to be in love, a feeling divine
feeling so pure, lovers ever, on cloud nine;

Sometime I reflect, what this love could be
if love be blind, what a bliss, would it be
bereft of logic and contrive, would it be
content to surrender, seek naught, would it be;

I pray to thee, my Master
in thy shadow, allow me for ever
let purity, be embedded in my mind
lead me to thee, though my love be blind.

***

96
Crystal Gazing

I stretch my imagination, to the future that be
I crystal gaze my life, beyond the life, to see
I look in the crystal ball, in trance, I may not be
I tickle my thoughts, but not to make a prophecy;

Neither a forecast nor a prediction, do I try
I fancy my future, at many a stage, of my life
my thoughts change and so do the dreams, that be
as I grow, my experience in life, changes my fantasy;

When young, full of energy, I was inspired to be
to skip many a stage in life and rise instantaneously
bored with the school, I would envy the animal life
to be a canine pet, no studies, all pamper, yet a dog's life;

Sometimes I would think, of the life feline
pretty dames, cosying, fondling, all the time
but I would have many moods, hard to understand
what if I were not a pet, life, would not be so grand;

I would often be enamoured, by the life equine
majestic in looks and graceful in my stride
adrenaline flowing, would be galloping, all the time
but harsh would be my fate, when I be past my prime;

The time has now gone by, I have experienced life
I recollect and gaze back, at my struggle and strife
what life has given me and what I wished it to be
a life of love, to live this life, to be in, yet not, indeed;

I crystal gaze now, but I have very little time
what be my fancy, I have to make up my mind
I sit back and reflect, on the futility of this life
painful to relive, yet again, through all this grind;

The sensitivity, emotions, aspirations, fulfilled and not
the pleasure and pain of love, the love I found, the love I lost
the stress, the strain, the struggle and what has it brought
not worth a life time, I rather be out of this cycle, is my thought
if it cannot be, then human it not be, whatever else he may allot.

***

97

The Last Mile

I am the toughest, I am the harshest
I may not be, but I appear the longest
when in sight, they break into a smile
too distant at the start, I am the last mile;

For some, I am the home stretch
for some, a stretch away from home
for some, I am beginning of the end
for some, I am end of the commencement;

Myriad are my shades, a matter of perception
I connect people with people, to their destination
like blood through the veins, the capillaries, I reach the ends
like nourishment to the leaves, I am the route, through the stem;

Long I may be, yet undeniably I am the chapter last
of the play, the story, the project, once the die is cast
they start with vigour, peak, but are not so, in the last lap
exhausted in energy and their will, there lies the catch;

It takes a champion, to plan the run, in the last mile
to fight to the finish and not hold back, to rest a while
squeeze every ounce of energy, for the last ditch stand
intense be the concentration, to play the game as planned;

To some, the last mile is akin, to the journey of life
curiously I observe, the psyche of those in their twilight
brooding the life past, engulfed by fear of the unknown
staring at the writing on the wall, to walk the last mile alone;

I stretch my imagination, if I were to plan my own last mile
strange, I find, life is but a series of many a last mile
each stage, each project, each competition is a test by design
built-in these have, own beginnings and last laps assigned;

I sit back and reflect, to view life as a whole
in this long journey, short sprints, matter no more
I decide to live at my own pace, to take the events in my stride
treat every day as the last and live this life, from mile to mile.

***

98

How Green Was My Valley

A beautiful line, a novel, a movie, a song
but to a beautiful valley, I too once did belong
born in the lush green meadow, of the vale
I grew up in the splashing sunshine, of the dale;

Daffodils, hydrangeas, dotting the scene
walnut, chinar, willow, poplar, all to be seen
meandering paths, snaking from end to end
affectionate people, to reach out, was the trend;

Apples, almonds, cherries to blossom
cradle of love it was, from top to bottom
peace and harmony, oozing from within
a paradise on earth, the valley, was akin;

Time passed well, until events took charge
undercurrents of discord, and all was lost
vandalism seethed in, in the name of God
bloodbath started, from across, was the call;

Hordes of them, would sneak in with stealth
sway the innocent, to rise, stones would they pelt
armed to the teeth, the mercenaries were there
enticing the youth, alienated, but little did they care;

Not easy to stem the deluge, whoever held the reins
lured would be the youth, to go across and train
all topsy- turvy, life came to a grinding halt
none did gain, even the perpetrators, from across;

Soft targets, the people, buildings, shrines
not an inch forward, all pushed back in time
confused in mind, know not what they want
most sit on the fence, peace still playing truant;

I pray to God, let good sense prevail
let the old times be back, retracing the trail
let me go back, to my meadow in the vale
let my valley be green once again.

***

99

Picking up Threads

I pick up the threads, from my life's spread
can hardly remember, from where had I left
conflict in my thoughts, wither to recommence
hazy is the memory, random is the access;

Memories, buried deep within
I scratch the surface, some mist is lifting
so many are the layers, can hardly decide
soon the haze is gone, and memories come alive;

Picking up threads, I walk down the memory lane
I fondly recall my early days, simple life, nothing at stake
aspirations high, shining like a star, glint in the eye
to soar like a bird, be someone and reach for the sky;

Sights set high, but the path not so bright
hurdles many, some I could not pass by
finally the plateau, in the curve of my life
my potential controlling the level of my rise;

I vividly recall, the memories of my love
innocent, pure, my cherished treasure trove
you in my thoughts, residing all the time
spurred to life I was, in rhythm and rhyme;

Warm was thy touch, reassuring thy presence
walking hand in hand, love was the essence
in bliss were we together, but it was not to be
soon were thee gone, reason unknown to me;

I fumbled, I stumbled, I was lost for a while
I picked up the threads, lady luck did smile
breaking from my past, I recharged ahead
my heart synergized, as my mind refreshed;

Long has been this journey, much water has flown
happy moments some, pain too has alongside grown
I smile, why reminisce what may not be, I dread
if I cannot relive my past, why pick up its threads.

***

100

I Await Thy Reply

When I could bear it no more
I chose not to keep it on a hold
a letter, pouring my heart and soul
with shaky hands, I penned my love in bold;

The post, hopefully, carried it afar
on foot, by air, train or by car
I hope the man did deliver it to thee
all my love, that I put down so tenderly;

Thence the wait started, with patience I was hoping
thy fragrance preceding, thee may be in the offing
hiding behind my shyness, I merely sought a reply
unsure how I ought to be, if thee chose to come by;

Awaiting thy response, I know not yet thy mind
be left to myself, or be exalted in my love divine
whether my love will be requited, or otherwise
to be in heavenly bliss, or destined to just live by;

Hesitant, yet throwing caution overboard
I had said it all, with my heart and soul
I wondered, if I had overstepped my line
how to retract, if thy love was not to be mine;

They say, love is mystery and a feeling apart
none think and calculate, in matters of the heart
I could not wait to write, lest it be too late
risky though, if it be a no, but all did I state;

Sometimes I fancy, my letter may strike a chord
triggering thy love for me, if dormant in thy heart
blessed are those, who have their love requited in life
how I wish, I too could be half as lucky, if not twice;

Strange thoughts do cross my mind, besides
let there be no reply, if it has to be, otherwise
hope would ever keep thy memory alive
reassured within, I still wait for thy reply.

***